PROGRAMMER COLLECTION

UNIX® System V

Understanding ELF Object Files and Debugging Tools

Edited by
Mary Lou Nohr

P T R Prentice Hall
Englewood Cliffs, New Jersey 07632

PRENTICE HALL OPEN SYSTEMS LIBRARY

UNIX system V : understanding ELF object files and debugging tools /
edited by Mary Lou Nohr.
p. cm. -- (Prentice Hall open systems library)
Includes bibliographical references and index.
ISBN 0-13-091109-7
1. UNIX System V (Computer files) 2. File organization (Computer science)
3. Debugging in computer science. I. Nohr, Mary Lou.
II. Series.
Qa76.76.063U5521[redacted] 1994
005.4'53--dc20

93-37472
CIP

Editorial/production supervision: *Ann Sullivan*
Cover design: *Eloise Starkweather*
Manufacturing buyer: *Alexis Heydt*
Acquisition editor: *Phyllis Eve Bregman*
Editorial assistant: *Nancy Boylan*
Cover art: *Rolling* (Adolf Gottlieb). (From Virginia Museum of Fine Arts, Richmond. Gift of Sydney and Frences Lewis)

Published by P T R Prentice Hall
Prentice-Hall, Inc.
A Paramount Communications Company
Englewood Cliffs, New Jersey 07632

The publisher offers discounts on this book when ordered in bulk quantities. For more information contact:

Corporate Sales Department
P T R Prentice Hall
113 Sylvan Avenue
Englewood Cliffs, NJ 07632

Phone: 201-592-2863
Fax: 201-592-2249

Printed in the United States of America
10 9 8 7 6 5 4 3 2 1

ISBN 0-13-091109-7

Prentice-Hall International (UK) Limited, *London*
Prentice-Hall of Australia Pty. Limited, *Sydney*
Prentice-Hall Canada Inc., *Toronto*
Prentice-Hall Hispanoamericana, S.A.,
Prentice-Hall of India Private Limited, *New Delhi*
Prentice-Hall of Japan, Inc., *Tokyo*
Simon & Schuster Asia Pte. Ltd., *Singapore*
Editora Prentice-Hall do Brasil, Ltda., *Rio de Janeiro*

Table of Contents

List of Figures

List of Tables

Preface

The book *Understanding ELF Object Files and Debugging Tools* brings together in one source the pieces of the UNIX System V Release 4 compilation and operating system that provide information about the Executable and Linking Format (ELF) object files: their formation, their elements, their structure, their manipulation by calls to ELF library functions, their accessibility for study and modification by programmers, their debugging, and their influence on active processes.

The book is intended for compiler writers, as most application programmers are unconcerned with the inner workings of ELF object files. Nevertheless, the latter group can benefit from an increased understanding of the dynamics of object files in program linking and execution.

❑ Summary of Contents

Chapter 1, "Overview," reviews the C compilation system, including dynamic linking and the product of compilation, `a.out` or the ELF object file. The chapter presents a rationale for dynamic linking.

Chapter 2, "Program Linking," looks at object files from the linking view. It describes object file information and system actions that create static program representations from relocatable files and shared objects.

Chapter 3, "Program Execution," examines the other view of object files — execution. The chapter describes object file structure as it relates to program execution. The chapter discusses program loading, the program interpreter, and the dynamic linker.

Chapter 4, "ELF Library Functions," describes the functions that allow programs to access and manipulate object files. The functions are contained in `libelf.h`.

Chapter 5 "UNIX Tools for ELF Files," describes the UNIX commands for file or library conversion, retrieval of file information, and file manipulation.

Chapter 6, "Source-level Debugging with `sdb`," describes debugging techniques for post-mortem debugging (debugging a core file) and for live process debugging.

Chapter 7, "System Traces," discusses the `/proc` file system and the `truss` command, which allow programmers to trace active processes, system calls, machine faults, and so forth.

Appendix A, "System Call Error Returns," presents error numbers and descriptions.

Appendix B, "Signal References," provides information about signals that relates to debugging object files and tracing processes.

❑ Related Reading

UNIX System V Release 4 Programming in Standard C, UNIX System Laboratories, Prentice Hall, Englewood Cliffs NJ, ISBN: 0-13-017666-4.

UNIX System V Release 4 Programmer's Reference Manual: Operating System API, UNIX System Laboratories, Prentice Hall, Englewood Cliffs, NJ, ISBN: 0-13-951294-2.

UNIX System V Release 4 User's Reference Manual/ System Administrator's Reference Manual (two volumes), UNIX System Laboratories, Prentice Hall, Englewood Cliffs, NJ: ISBN: Commands a-l: 0-13-951310-8; Commands m-z: 0-13-9511328-0.

UNIX System V Release 4 System Files and Devices Reference Manual, UNIX System Laboratories, Prentice Hall, Englewood Cliffs, NJ: ISBN: 0-13-951302-7.

UNIX System V Release 4 Application Binary Interface, UNIX System Laboratories, Prentice Hall, Englewood Cliffs NJ, ISBN: 0-13-100439-5.

❑ Conventions

The following notational conventions are used in the text.

Italics represents placeholders in command and variables for context-sensitive values like file names, device type and names, numeric values, and so forth.

`Courier` is used for literal commands and options, file names, and output from the computer.

A carriage return at the end of each command is implied. When a command extends beyond the width of the page, the break is marked with a backslash and an indented second line:

```
$ cc -L../archives -L../mylibs file1.c file2.c file3.c \
    file4.c -lfoo
```

Of course, a command that extends beyond the width of the terminal screen wraps around. You should use the backslash only if you enter the command exactly as shown.

`#` (pound sign) is the default system prompt for the root or superuser.

`$` (dollar sign) is the default system prompt for the ordinary user.

◆ Notes contain remarks slightly off the subject at hand but still pertinent to the discussion.

▼ Cautions warn of potential dangers.

Other conventions used in the text are as follows:

- ▲ In cases where you are expected to enter a control character, the character is shown as, for example, `control_d` or `^d`. Either form means that you depress the `d` key while holding down the `CTRL` key.
- ▲ A number in parentheses following a command or function name refers to the section of the reference manuals where the command or function is described. For example, `cc`(1), means that the `cc` command is described in Section 1 of the reference manuals.

❑ Acknowledgments

This book is derived from information in the UNIX System V Release 4 books listed in "Related Reading." While the material has been rearranged, reworked, and edited, it retains much of the flavor and many of the words of the original material.

Many thanks to Elka Grisham and Bill Klinger from UNIX System Laboratories for their continuous support during this project. Thanks also to Phyllis Eve Bregman, my editor at PTR Prentice Hall, and to Ron Gomes for reviewing the manuscript.

1

Overview

This chapter provides the setting for the processes described in the rest of the book. It presents an overview of the C compilation system, especially the link editor, and defines the entities of header files and object files with respect to file format and data representation.

❑ The C Compilation System

The C compilation system consists of a compiler, assembler, and link editor. The `cc` command invokes each of these components automatically unless you use command line options to specify otherwise. [See `cc`(1) for details of the options.] Figure 1-1 shows the organization of the C compilation system. Details concerning the optional optimizer are omitted.

Figure 1-1
Organization of C Compilation System

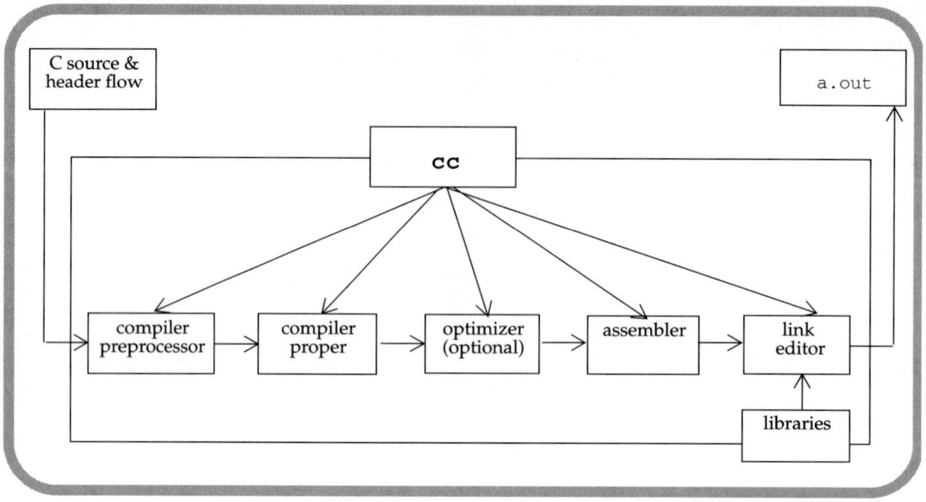

An executable C program is created with the following four steps:

1. The preprocessor component of the compiler reads lines in source files that direct it to replace a name with a token string (`#define`), perhaps conditionally (`#if`, for example). It also accepts directives in source files to include the contents of a named file in a program (`#include`). Included header files for the most part consist of `#define` directives and declarations of external symbols, definitions and declarations that you want to make available to more than one source file.
2. The compiler proper translates the C language code in the source files, which now contain the preprocessed contents of any included header files, into assembly language code.
3. The assembler translates the assembly language code into the machine instructions of the computer on which a program is to run. These instructions are stored in object files that correspond to each of the source files. Each object file contains a binary representation of the C language code in the corresponding source file. Object files are made up of sections, usually at least two in number. The text section consists mainly of program instructions. Text sections normally have read and execute, but not write, permissions. Data sections normally have read, write, and execute permissions.
4. The link editor links these object files with each other and with any library functions called in the program. When it links with the library functions depends on the link editing model you have chosen.

a. An archive, or statically linked library, is a collection of object files each of which contains the code for a function or a group of related functions in the library. When you use a library function in a program and specify a static linking option on the `cc` command line, a copy of the object file that contains the function is incorporated in your executable at link time.

b. A shared object, or dynamically linked library, is a single object file that contains the code for every function in the library. When you call a library function in a program and specify a dynamic linking option on the `cc` command line, the entire contents of the shared object are mapped into the virtual address space of your process at runtime. As its name implies, a shared object contains code that can be used simultaneously by different programs at runtime.

The default `cc` command line

```
$ cc file1.c file2.c file3.c
```

creates object files corresponding to each of the source files and links them with each other to create an executable program. These object files are called relocatable object files because they contain references to symbols that have not yet been connected with their definitions; that is, have not yet been assigned addresses in memory.

❑ Header Files

Header files serve as the interface between a program and the libraries supplied by the C compilation system. Because the functions that perform standard I/O often use the same definitions and declarations, the system supplies a common interface to the functions in the header file `stdio.h`. To make definitions or declarations available to several source files, you can create a header file with any editor, store it in a convenient directory, and include it in a program.

Header files traditionally are designated by the suffix `.h` and are brought into a program at compile time. The preprocessor component of the compiler interprets certain # statements in a program as directives. The two most commonly used directives are `#include` and `#define`. The `#include` directive calls in and processes the contents of the named file. The `#define` directive defines the replacement token string for an identifier. For example,

```
#define NULL   0
```

defines the macro `NULL` to have the replacement token sequence `0`. When you use a library function in a program, you can consult the manual page regarding which header file, if any, should be included. If a header file is mentioned, then include it before you use any of the associated functions or declarations in your program. Put the `#include` at the top of a source file.

❑ Link Editor

Link editing refers to the process in which a symbol referenced in one module of a program is connected with its definition in another. Whichever link editing model — static or dynamic — a programmer chooses, the link editor searches each module of the program, including any saved libraries that are used, for definitions of undefined external symbols in the other modules. If it does not find a definition for a symbol, then the link editor reports an error by default and fails to create an executable program.

Symbols with multiple definitions— except for different-sized initialized data objects — are not reported as errors under dynamic linking. The link editor does not report an error for multiple definitions of a function or a same-sized data object when each such definition resides within a different shared object or within a dynamically linked executable and different shared objects. In contrast, multiply defined symbols are generally reported as errors under static linking, because definitions of so-called weak symbols can be hidden from the link editor by a definition of a global symbol.

The principal difference between static and dynamic linking lies in what happens after the search is completed:

- ▲ Under static linking, copies of the archive library object files that satisfy still unresolved external references in a program are incorporated in the executable at link time. External references in the program are connected with their definitions — assigned addresses in memory — when the executable is created.
- ▲ Under dynamic linking, the contents of a shared object are mapped into the virtual address space of a process at runtime. External refer-

ences in a program are connected with their definitions when the program is executed.

The Case for Dynamic Linking

You might prefer dynamic linking to static linking for these reasons.

- Dynamically linked programs save disk storage and system process memory by sharing library code at runtime. Because shared object code is not copied into an executable object file at link time, a dynamically linked executable normally uses less disk space than a statically linked executable uses.
- Dynamically linked code can be fixed or enhanced without the need to relink applications that depend on it. Shared object code can be changed without breaking executables that depend on it. Even if a shared C library were enhanced in the future, you would not have to relink programs that depended on it as long as the enhancements were compatible with your code.

In a few cases, you might not want to use dynamic linking.

- If a program calls only a few small library functions, the bookkeeping information to be used by the dynamic linker may take up more space in the executable than the code for those functions does. You can use the `size` command (see Chapter 5) to determine the difference.
- Similarly, using a shared object can occasionally add to the memory requirements of a process. Although a shared object's text is shared by all processes that use it, its writable data typically are not shared. Every process that uses a shared object usually gets a private copy of its entire data segment, regardless of how much of the data are needed. If an application uses only a small portion of a shared library's text and data, then executing the application might require more memory with a shared object than without one.

Specification of Dynamic Linking

By convention, shared objects, or dynamically linked libraries, are designated by the prefix `lib` and the suffix `.so`; archives, or statically linked libraries, are designated by the prefix `lib` and the suffix `.a`. Then, `libc.so` is the shared object version of the standard C library; `libc.a` is the archive version.

These conventions are recognized, in turn, by the `-l` option to the `cc` command. That is, the command

```
$ cc file1.c file2.c file3.c -lx
```

directs the link editor to search the shared object `libx.so` or the archive library `libx.a`. The `cc` command automatically passes `-lc` to the link editor.

By default, the link editor chooses the shared object implementation of a library, `libx.so`, in preference to the archive library implementation, `libx.a`, in the same directory. Under the default arrangement, the `cc` command creates and then links relocatable object files to generate an executable program, then arranges for the executable to be linked with the shared C library at runtime. If you are satisfied with this arrangement, you need make no other provision for link editing on the `cc` command line.

When you use the `-l` option to link your program with `libfoo.so`

```
$ cc -Ldir file1.c file2.c file3.c -lfoo
```

the link editor records in your executable the name of the shared object and a small amount of bookkeeping information for use by the system at runtime. Another component of the system — the dynamic linker — does the actual linking. The dynamic linker simply uses the definitions in the new version of the library to resolve external references in the executables at runtime.

To force an executable to be linked with the archive version of all libraries being searched, specify the `-dn` option on the `cc` command line. [See `cc`(1) for other overrides.]

❑ Object Files

Created by the assembler and link editor, object files (`a.out`) are binary representations of programs intended to execute directly on a processor. The three main types of object files are:

- A *relocatable file* — holds code and data suitable for linking with other object files to create an executable or a shared object file.
- An *executable file* — holds a program suitable for execution; the file specifies how `exec`(2) creates a program's process image.
- A *shared object file* — holds code and data suitable for linking in two contexts. First, the link editor processes the shared object file with other relocatable and shared object files to create another object file. Second, the dynamic linker combines it with an executable file and other shared objects to create a process image.

Programs that need to access and manipulate object files do so by means of functions contained in the ELF access library, `libelf.h`. (See "Elf Library Functions" in Chapter 4 for more information.)

The Output File, `a.out`

The file name `a.out` is the default output file name from the link editor, `ld`. The link editor makes an `a.out` file executable if no errors in linking occurred.

When an `a.out` file is loaded into memory for execution, three logical segments are set up: the text segment, the data segment (initialized data followed by uninitialized data, the latter actually being initialized to all zeros), and a stack.

The text segment is not writable by the program; if other processes are executing the same `a.out` file, then the processes share a single text segment.

The data segment starts at the next maximal page boundary past the last text address. If the system supports more than one page size, then the "maximal page" is the largest supported size.

When the process image is created, the part of the file holding the end of text and the beginning of data may appear twice. The duplicated chunk of text that appears at the beginning of data is never executed; it is duplicated so that the operating system can bring in pieces of the file in multiples of the actual page size without having to realign the beginning of the data section to a page boundary. Therefore, the first data address is the sum of the next maximal page boundary past the end of text plus the remainder of the last text address divided by the maximal page size. If the last text address is a multiple of the maximal page size, no duplication is necessary.

The stack is automatically extended as required. The data segment is extended as requested by the `brk`(2) system call.

File Format

Object files participate in program linking (building a program) and program execution (running a program). For convenience and efficiency, the object file format provides parallel views of a file's contents, reflecting the differing needs of these activities.

Figure 1-2 shows object file organization.

Figure 1-2
Object File Format
Although the figure shows the program header table immediately after the ELF header, and the section header table following the sections, actual files may differ. Only the ELF header has a fixed position in the file.

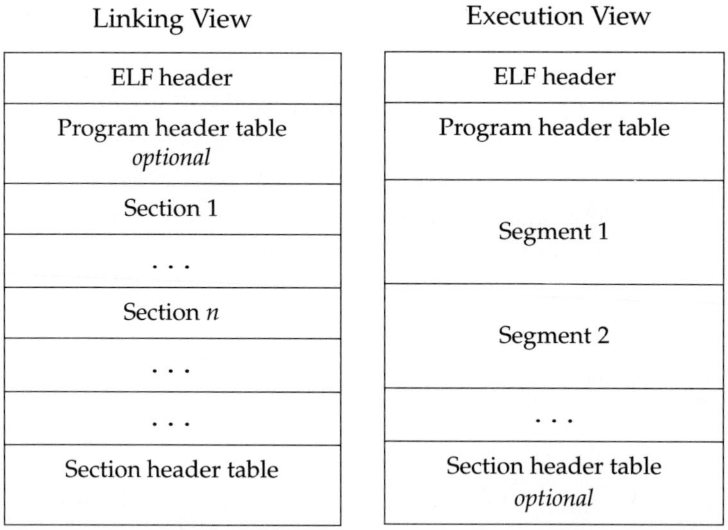

An ELF *header*, which resides at the beginning of the file, holds a "road map" describing the file's organization. *Sections* hold the bulk of object file information for the linking view: instructions data, symbol table, relocation information, and so on. (Chapter 2 discusses sections and the program linking view of the file.) *Segments* hold the object file information for the program execution view. As shown, a segment can contain one or more sections. (Chapter 3 discusses segments and the program execution view of the file.)

A *program header table* tells the system how to create a process image from the ELF object. In the program execution view, files used to build a process image (execute a program) must have a program header table; relocatable files do not need one.

A *section header table* contains information describing the file sections. Every section has an entry in the table; each entry provides information such as the section name, the section size, and so forth. Files used during linking must have a section header table; other object files may or may not have one.

Data Representation

Conceptually, two parallel sets of objects support cross compilation environments. One set corresponds to file contents, while the other set corresponds to the native memory image of the program manipulating the file. Type definitions supplied by the header files work on the native machine, which may have different data encodings (size, byte order, and so forth) than the target machine. Although native memory objects should be at least as big as the file objects (to avoid information loss), they may be bigger, if that is more natural for the host machine.

As described here, the object file format supports various processors with 8-bit bytes and 32-bit architectures, but it is extensible to larger (or smaller) architectures. Object files therefore represent some control data with a machine-independent format, making it possible to identify object files and interpret their contents in a common way. Remaining data in an object file use the encoding of the target processor, regardless of the machine on which the file was created.

Table 1-1 summarizes the 32-bit data types.

Table 1-1 *32-Bit Data Types*

Name	Size	Alignment	Purpose
`Elf32_Addr`	4	4	Unsigned program address
`Elf32_Half`	2	2	Unsigned medium integer
`Elf32_Off`	4	4	Unsigned file offset
`Elf32_Sword`	4	4	Signed large integer
`Elf32_Word`	4	4	Unsigned large integer
unsigned char	1	1	Unsigned small integer

All data structures that the object file format defines follow the "natural" size and alignment guidelines for the relevant class. If necessary, data structures contain explicit padding to ensure 4-byte alignment for 4-byte objects, to force structure sizes to a multiple of 4, and so forth. Data also have suitable alignment from the beginning of the file. For example, a structure containing an `Elf32_Addr` member will be aligned on a 4-byte boundary within the file.

For portability, ELF uses no bit-fields.

2

Program Linking

The "linking" view of an object file, illustrated in Figure 1-2, includes an ELF header, sections, and a section header table. This chapter describes those entities; the optional program header table is discussed in Chapter 3.

This chapter also describes the object file information and system actions that create static program representations from relocatable files and shared objects.

❑ ELF Header

Some object file control structures can grow, because the ELF header contains their actual sizes. If the object file format changes, then a program can encounter control structures that are larger or smaller than expected. Programs might, therefore, ignore "extra" information. The treatment of "missing" information depends on context and will be specified when and if extensions are defined.

Figure 2-1 illustrates ELF header structure.

Figure 2-1
ELF Header Structure

```
#define EI_NIDENT       16

typedef struct {
        unsigned char   e_ident[EI_NIDENT];
        Elf32_Half      e_type;
        Elf32_Half      e_machine;
        Elf32_Word      e_version;
        Elf32_Addr      e_entry;
        Elf32_Off       e_phoff;
        Elf32_Off       e_shoff;
        Elf32_Word      e_flags;
        Elf32_Half      e_ehsize;
        Elf32_Half      e_phentsize;
        Elf32_Half      e_phnum;
        Elf32_Half      e_shentsize;
        Elf32_Half      e_shnum;
        Elf32_Half      e_shstrndx;
} Elf32_Ehdr;
```

The members have the following meaning.

`e_ident` The initial bytes mark the file as an object file and provide machine-independent data with which to decode and interpret the file contents. Complete descriptions are provided in "ELF Identification" on page 15.

`e_type` Identifies the object file type, as shown in Table 2-1.

Table 2-1 *Object File Types*

Name	Value	Meaning
ET_NONE	0	No file type
ET_REL	1	Relocatable file
ET_EXEC	2	Executable file
ET_DYN	3	Shared object file
ET_CORE	4	Core file
ET_LOPROC	0xff00	Processor-specific
ET_HIPROC	0xffff	Processor-specific

Although the core file contents are unspecified in the *System V Application Binary Interface*, type ET_CORE is reserved to mark the file. Values from ET_LOPROC through ET_HIPROC (inclusive) are reserved for processor-specific semantics. Other values are reserved and will be assigned to new object file types as necessary.

e_machine

Value specifies the required architecture for an individual file. The types are listed in Table 2-2.

Table 2-2 *Machine Names for Specific Architectures*

Name	Value	Meaning
EM_NONE	0	No machine
EM_M32	1	AT&T WE 32100
EM_SPARC	2	SPARC®
EM_386	3	Intel386™ CPU
EM_68K	4	Motorola 68000
EM_88K	5	Motorola 88000
EM_860	7	Intel860™ CPU
EM_MIPS	8	MIPS R2000

Other values are reserved and will be assigned to new machines as necessary. Processor-specific ELF names use the machine name to distinguish them.

e_version

Identifies the object file version, as listed in Table 2-3.

Table 2-3 *Object File Versions*

Name	Value	Meaning
EV_NONE	0	Invalid version
EV_CURRENT	1	Current version

The value 1 signifies the original file format; extensions create new versions with higher numbers. Although the value of EV_CURRENT is shown as 1 in the preceding table, it changes as necessary to reflect the current version number.

`e_entry` Holds the virtual address to which the system first transfers control, thus starting the process. If the file has no associated entry point, then this member holds zero.

`e_phoff` Holds the file offset, in bytes, of the program header table. If the file has no program header table, then this member holds zero.

`e_shoff` Holds the file offset, in bytes, of the section header table. If the file has no section header table, then this member holds zero.

`e_flags` Holds processor-specific flags associated with the file. Flag names take the form `EF_`*machine*_flag.

`e_ehsize` Holds the ELF header size in bytes.

`e_phentsize`
Holds the size in bytes of one entry in the file's program header table; all entries are the same size.

`e_phnum` Holds the number of entries in the program header table. Thus, the product of `e_phentsize` and `e_phnum` gives the table size in bytes. If a file has no program header table, then `e_phnum` holds the value zero.

`e_shentsize`
Holds a section header's size in bytes. A section header is one entry in the section header table; all entries are the same size.

`e_shnum` Holds the number of entries in the section header table. Thus, the product of `e_shentsize` and `e_shnum` gives the size of the section header table in bytes. If a file has no section header table, then `e_shnum` holds the value zero.

`e_shstrndx`
Holds the section header table index of the entry associated with the section name string table. If the file has no section name string table, then `e_shstrndx` holds the value

SHN_UNDEF. (See "Sections" on page 18 and "String Table" on page 30 for more information.)

ELF Identification

ELF provides an object file framework to support multiple processors, multiple data encodings, and multiple classes of machines. To support this object file family, the initial bytes of the file specify how to interpret the file, independently of the processor on which the inquiry is made and independently of the remaining contents of the file.

The initial bytes of an ELF header (and an object file) correspond to the e_ident member, listed in Table 2-4.

Table 2-4 ***e_ident[ ] Identification Indexes***

Name	Value	Purpose
EI_MAG0	0	File identification
EI_MAG1	1	File identification
EI_MAG2	2	File identification
EI_MAG3	3	File identification
EI_CLASS	4	File class
EI_DATA	5	Data encoding
EI_VERSION	6	File version
EI_PAD	7	Start of padding bytes
EI_NIDENT	16	Size of e_ident[]

The indexes access bytes that hold the following values.

EI_MAG0 to EI_MAG3
: Hold a "magic number," identifying the file as an ELF object file, as listed in Table 2-5.

Table 2-5 ***ELF File Identifier***

Name	Value	Position
ELFMAG0	0x7f	e_ident[EI_MAG0]
ELFMAG1	'E'	e_ident[EI_MAG1]

Table 2-5 *ELF File Identifier (Continued)*

Name	Value	Position
ELFMAG2	'L'	e_ident[EI_MAG2]
ELFMAG3	'F'	e_ident[EI_MAG3]

EI_CLASS

Identifies the file class, or capacity, as listed in Table 2-6.

Table 2-6 *ELF File Class Identifier*

Name	Value	Meaning
ELFCLASSNONE	0	Invalid class
ELFCLASS32	1	32-bit objects
ELFCLASS64	2	64-bit objects

The file format is portable among machines of various sizes, without imposing the sizes of the largest machine on the smallest. Class ELFCLASS32 supports machines with files and virtual address spaces up to 4 gigabytes and uses the basic types defined in the previous table.

Class ELFCLASS64 is reserved for 64-bit architectures. Its appearance here shows how the object file can change, but the 64-bit format is otherwise unspecified. Other classes will be defined as necessary, with different basic types and sizes for object file data.

EI_DATA Specifies the data encoding of the processor-specific data in the object file. The currently defined encodings are shown in the table below.

Table 2-7 *Data Encodings*

Name	Value	Meaning
ELFDATANONE	0	Invalid data encoding
ELFDATA2LSB	1	See Figure 2-2
ELFDATA2MSB	2	See Figure 2-3

Other values are reserved and will be assigned to new encodings as necessary.

EI_VERSION
Specifies the ELF header version number. Currently, this value must be EV_CURRENT, for e_version.

EI_PAD
Marks the beginning of the unused bytes in e_ident. These bytes are reserved and set to zero; programs that read object files should ignore them. The value of EI_PAD will change in the future if currently unused bytes are given meanings.

A file's data encoding specifies how to interpret the basic objects in a file. Class ELFCLASS32 files use objects that occupy 1, 2, and 4 bytes. Under the defined encodings, objects are represented as detailed in Figure 2-2. Byte numbers appear in the upper left corners.

Encoding ELFDATA2LSB specifies 2's complement values, with the least significant byte occupying the lowest address.

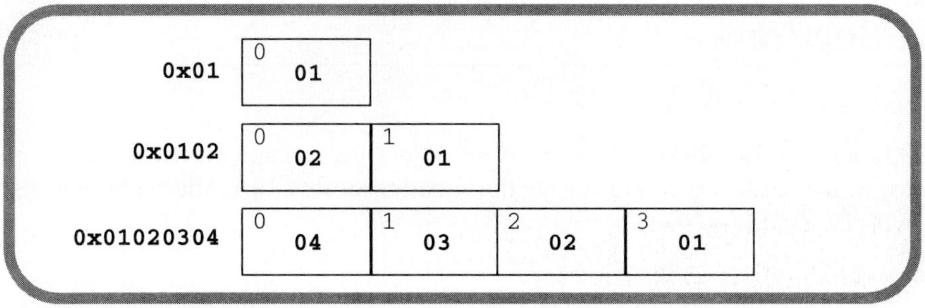

Figure 2-2 *Data Encoding* ***ELFDATA2LSB*** *Byte numbers are shown in the upper left corners.*

Encoding ELFDATA2MSB specifies 2's complement values, with the most significant byte occupying the lowest address, as shown in Figure 2-3.

Figure 2-3 *Data Encoding* ***ELFDATA2MSB*** *Byte numbers are shown in the upper left corners.*

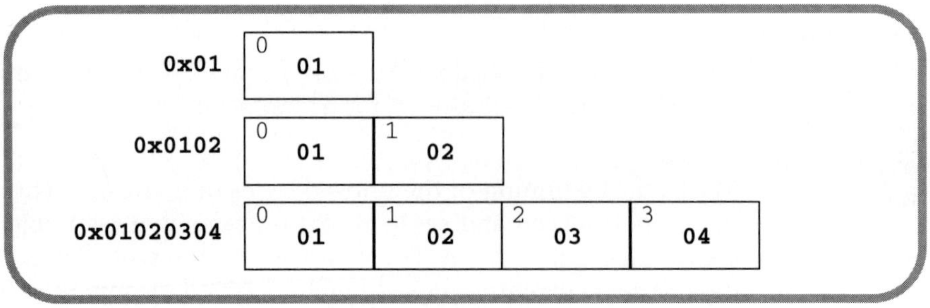

ELF Header Flags

The ELF header `e_flags` member holds bit flags associated with the file. ELF header flags are machine-specific. The ABI supplement for the desired processor describes the details.

❑ Sections

Sections contain all information in an object file except the ELF header, the program header table, and the section header table. Object file sections satisfy several conditions.

- ▲ Every section in an object file has exactly one section header describing it. Section headers might exist that do not have a section.
- ▲ Each section occupies one contiguous (possibly empty) sequence of bytes within a file.
- ▲ Sections in a file cannot overlap. No byte in a file resides in more than one section.
- ▲ An object file can have inactive space. The various headers and the sections might not cover every byte in an object file. The contents of the inactive data are unspecified.

Section Header

The section header table of an object file allows you to locate all the file sections. The section header table is an array of Elf32_Shdr structures as described in Figure 2-4. A section header table index is a subscript into this array. Some section header table indexes are reserved; an object file will not have sections for these special indexes. (See "Reserved Header Table Indexes" on page 25.)

The ELF header's e_shoff member gives the byte offset from the beginning of the file to the section header table. e_shnum tells how many entries the section header table contains. e_shentsize gives the size in bytes of each entry.

A section header has the structure shown in Figure 2-4.

Figure 2-4 *Section Header Structure*

```
typedef struct {
        Elf32_Word        sh_name;
        Elf32_Word        sh_type;
        Elf32_Word        sh_flags;
        Elf32_Addr        sh_addr;
        Elf32_Off         sh_offset;
        Elf32_Word        sh_size;
        Elf32_Word        sh_link;
        Elf32_Word        sh_info;
        Elf32_Word        sh_addralign;
        Elf32_Word        sh_entsize;
} Elf32_Shdr;
```

The members have the following meaning.

sh_name — Specifies the name of the section. Its value is an index into the section header string table section, giving the location of a null-terminated string. (See "String Table" on page 30 for more information.)

sh_type — Categorizes the section's contents and semantics. Section types and their descriptions are listed in Table 2-8 on page 21.

`sh_flags` Sections support 1-bit flags that describe miscellaneous attributes. Flag definitions are listed in Table 2-9 on page 23.

`sh_addr` Gives the address at which the section's first byte should reside, if the section will appear in the memory image of a process. Otherwise, the member contains 0.

`sh_offset`
Gives the byte offset from the beginning of the file to the first byte in the section. One section type, `SHT_NOBITS` (see page 22), occupies no space in the file, and its `sh_offset` member locates the conceptual placement in the file.

`sh_size` Gives the section size in bytes. Unless the section type is `SHT_NOBITS`, the section occupies `sh_size` bytes in the file. A section of type `SHT_NOBITS` can have a non-zero size, but it occupies no space in the file.

`sh_link` Holds a section header table index link, whose interpretation depends on the section type. Table 2-10 on page 24 describes the values.

`sh_info` Holds extra information, whose interpretation depends on the section type. Table 2-10 describes the values.

`sh_addralign`
Some sections have address alignment constraints. For example, if a section holds a doubleword, then the system must ensure doubleword alignment for the entire section. The value of `sh_addr` must be congruent to 0, modulo the value of `sh_addralign`. Currently, only 0 and positive integral powers of two are allowed. Values 0 and 1 mean the section has no alignment constraints.

`sh_entsize`
Some sections hold a table of fixed-size entries, such as a symbol table. For such a section, this member gives the size in bytes of each entry. The member contains 0 if the section does not hold a table of fixed-size entries.

Section Header sh_type Member

A section header's sh_type member specifies the section's semantics.

Table 2-8 *Section Types, sh_type*

Name	Value
SHT_NULL	0
SHT_PROGBITS	1
SHT_SYMTAB	2
SHT_STRTAB	3
SHT_RELA	4
SHT_HASH	5
SHT_DYNAMIC	6
SHT_NOTE	7
SHT_NOBITS	8
SHT_REL	9
SHT_SHLIB	10
SHT_DYNSYM	11
SHT_LOPROC	0x70000000
SHT_HIPROC	0x7fffffff
SHT_LOUSER	0x80000000
SHT_HIUSER	0xffffffff

The types have the following meaning.

SHT_NULL Marks the section header as inactive; it does not have an associated section. Other members of the section header have undefined values.

SHT_PROGBITS
Holds information defined by the program, whose format and meaning are determined solely by the program.

SHT_SYMTAB and SHT_DYNSYM
Hold a symbol table. Currently, an object file can have only one section of each type, but this restriction may be relaxed in

the future. Typically, `SHT_SYMTAB` provides symbols for link editing, though it can also be used for dynamic linking. As a complete symbol table, it can contain many symbols unnecessary for dynamic linking. Consequently, an object file can also contain a `SHT_DYNSYM` section, which holds a minimal set of dynamic linking symbols, to save space. (See "Symbol Table" on page 31 for details.)

`SHT_STRTAB`
: Holds a string table. An object file can have multiple string table sections. (See "String Table" on page 30 for details.)

`SHT_RELA` Holds relocation entries with explicit addends, such as type `Elf32_Rela` for the 32-bit class of object files. An object file can have multiple relocation sections. (See "Relocation" on page 37 for details.)

`SHT_HASH` Holds a symbol hash table. All objects participating in dynamic linking must contain a symbol hash table. Currently, an object file can have only one hash table, but this restriction may be relaxed in the future.

`SHT_DYNAMIC`
: Holds information for dynamic linking. Currently, an object file can have only one dynamic section, but this restriction may be relaxed in the future.

`SHT_NOTE` Holds information that marks the file in some way.

`SHT_NOBITS`
: A section of this type occupies no space in the file but otherwise resembles `SHT_PROGBITS`. Although this section contains no bytes, the `sh_offset` member contains the conceptual file offset.

`SHT_REL` Holds relocation entries without explicit addends, such as type `Elf32_Rel` for the 32-bit class of object files. An object file can have multiple relocation sections. (See "Relocation" on page 37 for details.)

`SHT_SHLIB` Reserved, but has unspecified semantics.

SHT_LOPROC through SHT_HIPROC
Values in this inclusive range are reserved for processor-specific semantics.

SHT_LOUSER
Specifies the lower bound of the range of indexes reserved for application programs.

SHT_HIUSER
Specifies the upper bound of the range of indexes reserved for application programs. Section types between SHT_LOUSER and SHT_HIUSER can be used by the application without conflicting with current or future system-defined section types.

Other section type values are reserved. (See "Reserved Header Table Indexes" on page 25 for details.)

Section Header sh_flags Member

A section header's sh_flags member holds 1-bit flags that describe the section's attributes. If a flag bit is set in sh_flags, then the attribute is ON for the section. Otherwise, the attribute is OFF or does not apply. Undefined attributes are set to zero.

Defined values are listed in Table 2-9; other values are reserved.

Table 2-9 *Section Attribute Flags, sh_flags*

Name	Value
SHF_WRITE	0x1
SHF_ALLOC	0x2
SHF_EXECINSTR	0x4
SHF_MASKPROC	0xf0000000

The flags have the following meaning.

SHF_WRITE
: Contains data that should be writable during process execution.

SHF_ALLOC
: Occupies memory during process execution. Some control sections do not reside in the memory image of an object file; this attribute is off for those sections.

SHF_EXECINSTR
: Contains executable machine instructions.

SHF_MASKPROC
: All bits included in this mask are reserved for processor-specific semantics. If meanings are specified, then the processor supplement explains them.

Section Header sh_link and sh_info Members

Two members in the section header, sh_link and sh_info, hold special information, depending on section type, as listed in Table 2-10.

Table 2-10 *sh_link and sh_info Interpretation*

sh_type	sh_link	sh_info
SHT_DYNAMIC	The section header index of the string table used by entries in the section.	0
SHT_HASH	The section header index of the symbol table to which the hash table applies.	0
SHT_REL SHT_RELA	The section header index of the associated symbol table.	The section header index of the section to which the relocation applies.
SHT_SYMTAB SHT_DYNSYM	The section header index of the associated string table.	One greater than the symbol table index of the last local symbol (binding f4STB_LOCAL).
other	SHN_UNDEF	0

Reserved Header Table Indexes

Some section header table indexes are reserved; an object file will not have sections for these special indexes. lists the indexes.

Table 2-11 *Special Section Indexes*

Name	Value
SHN_UNDEF	0
SHN_LORESERVE	0xff00
SHN_LOPROC	0xff00
SHN_HIPROC	0xff1f
SHN_ABS	0xfff1
SHN_COMMON	0xfff2
SHN_HIRESERVE	0xffff

The indexes have the following meaning.

SHN_UNDEF

Marks an undefined, missing, irrelevant, or otherwise meaningless section reference. For example, a symbol "defined" relative to section number SHN_UNDEF is an undefined symbol. (See Table 2-12 on page 26 for details.)

Although index 0 is reserved as the undefined value, the section header table contains an entry for index 0. If the e_shnum member of the ELF header says a file has 6 entries in the section header table, then they have the indexes 0 through 5.

SHN_LORESERVE

Specifies the lower bound of the range of reserved indexes.

SHN_LOPROC through SHN_HIPROC

Values in this inclusive range are reserved for processor-specific semantics. If meanings are specified, the processor supplement explains them.

SHN_ABS Specifies absolute values for the corresponding reference. For example, symbols defined relative to section number SHN_ABS have absolute values and are not affected by relocation.

SHN_COMMON
Symbols defined relative to this section are common symbols, such as FORTRAN COMMON or unallocated C external variables.

SHN_HIRESERVE
Specifies the upper bound of the range of reserved indexes. The system reserves indexes between SHN_LORESERVE and SHN_HIRESERVE, inclusive; the values do not reference the section header table. The section header table does not contain entries for the reserved indexes.

The section header for index 0 (SHN_UNDEF) exists, even though the index marks undefined section references. This entry holds the following.

Table 2-12 *Section Header Entry: Index 0*

Name	Value	Note
sh_name	0	No name
sh_type	SHT_NULL	Inactive
sh_flags	0	No flags (see Table 2-9)
sh_addr	0	No address
sh_offset	0	No file offset
sh_size	0	No size
sh_link	SHN_UNDEF	No link information
sh_info	0	No auxiliary information
sh_addralign	0	No alignment
sh_entsize	0	No entries

Special Sections

Various sections hold program and control information. Table 2-13 shows sections that are used by the system; they have the indicated types and attributes.

Table 2-13 *Special Sections*

Name	Type	Attributes
.bss	SHT_NOBITS	SHF_ALLOC+SHF_WRITE
.comment	SHT_PROGBITS	none
.data	SHT_PROGBITS	SHF_ALLOC+SHF_WRITE
.data1	SHT_PROGBITS	SHF_ALLOC+SHF_WRITE
.debug	SHT_PROGBITS	none
.dynamic	SHT_DYNAMIC	see below
.dynstr	SHT_STRTAB	SHF_ALLOC
.dynsym	SHT_DYNSYM	SHF_ALLOC
.fini	SHT_PROGBITS	SHF_ALLOC+SHF_EXECINSTR
.got	SHT_PROGBITS	see below
.hash	SHT_HASH	SHF_ALLOC
.init	SHT_PROGBITS	SHF_ALLOC+SHF_EXECINSTR
.interp	SHT_PROGBITS	none
.line	SHT_PROGBITS	none
.note	SHT_NOTE	none
.plt	SHT_PROGBITS	see below
.rel*name*	SHT_REL	see below
.rela*name*	SHT_RELA	see below
.rodata	SHT_PROGBITS	SHF_ALLOC
.rodata1	SHT_PROGBITS	SHF_ALLOC
.shstrtab	SHT_STRTAB	none
.strtab	SHT_STRTAB	see below
.symtab	SHT_SYMTAB	see below
.text	SHT_PROGBITS	SHF_ALLOC+SHF_EXECINSTR

The sections have the following meaning.

`.bss` Holds uninitialized data that contribute to the program's memory image. By definition, the system initializes the data with zeros when the program begins to run. The section occupies no file space, as indicated by the section type, `SHT_NOBITS`.

`.comment` Holds version control information.

`.data` and `.data1`
Hold initialized data that contribute to the program's memory image.

`.debug` Holds information for symbolic debugging. The contents are unspecified. All section names with the prefix `.debug` are reserved for future use in the ABI.

`.dynamic` Holds dynamic linking information. The section's attributes will include the `SHF_ALLOC` bit. Whether the `SHF_WRITE` bit is set is processor specific. (See "Dynamic Linking" on page 53 for more information.)

`.dynstr` Holds strings needed for dynamic linking, most commonly the strings that represent the names associated with symbol table entries. (See"Dynamic Linking" on page 53 for more information.)

`.dynsym` Holds the dynamic linking symbol table. (See "Symbol Table" on page 31 for more information.)

`.fini` Holds executable instructions that contribute to the process termination code. When a program exits normally, the system arranges to execute the code in this section.

`.got` Holds the global offset table.

`.hash` Holds a symbol hash table.

`.init` Holds executable instructions that contribute to the process initialization code. When a program starts to run, the system arranges to execute the code in this section before calling the main program entry point (called `main` in C programs).

`.interp` Holds the path name of a program interpreter.

`.line` Holds line number information for symbolic debugging, which describes the correspondence between the source program and the machine code. The contents are unspecified.

`.note` Holds information in the format described in "Note Section" on page 48.

`.plt` Holds the procedure linkage table. (See "Global Offset Table and Procedure Linkage Table" on page 64 for more information.)

`.rel`*name* and `.rela`*name*
Hold relocation information, as described in "Relocation" on page 37. If the file has a loadable segment that includes relocation, then the sections' attributes include the `SHF_ALLOC` bit; otherwise, that bit will be off. Conventionally, *name* is supplied by the section to which the relocations apply. Thus, a relocation section for `.text` normally would have the name `.rel.text` or `.rela.text`.

`.rodata` and `.rodata1`
Hold read-only data that typically contribute to a non-writable segment in the process image. (See "Program Header" on page 42 for more information.)

`.shstrtab`
Holds section names.

`.strtab` Holds strings, most commonly the strings that represent the names associated with symbol table entries. If the file has a loadable segment that includes the symbol string table, the section attributes will include the `f4SHF_ALLOC` bit; otherwise, that bit will be off.

`.symtab` Holds a symbol table, as described in "Symbol Table" on page 31. If the file has a loadable segment that includes the symbol table, the section attributes include the `SHF_ALLOC` bit; otherwise, that bit will be off.

`.text` Holds the "text," or executable instructions, of program.

Section names with a dot (`.`) prefix are reserved for the system, although applications can use these sections if their existing meanings are satisfactory. Applications can use names without the prefix to avoid conflicts with system sections. The object file format allows you to define sections not shown in the previous list. An object file can have more than one section with the same name.

Section names reserved for a processor architecture are formed by placing an abbreviation of the architecture name ahead of the section name. The name should be taken from the architecture names used for `e_machine`. For example, `.FOO.psect` is the `psect` section defined by the FOO architecture. Existing extensions are called by their historical names.

❑ String Table

String table sections hold null-terminated character sequences, commonly called strings. The object file uses these strings to represent symbol and section names. You reference a string as an index into the string table section. The first byte, which is index zero, is defined to hold a null character. Likewise, a string table's last byte is defined to hold a null character, ensuring null termination for all strings. A string whose index is zero specifies either no name or a null name, depending on the context. An empty string table section is permitted; its section header's `sh_size` member would contain zero. Non-zero indexes are invalid for an empty string table.

A section header's `sh_name` member holds an index into the section header string table section, as designated by the `e_shstrndx` member of the ELF header. Figure 2-5 shows a string table with 25 bytes and the strings associated with various indexes.

Figure 2-5
String Table Example
A string table index can refer to any byte in the section. A string can appear more than once; references to substrings can exist; a single string can be referenced multiple times; unreferenced strings are allowed.

String Table

Index	+0	+1	+2	+3	+4	+5	+6	+7	+8	+9
0	\0	n	a	m	e	.	\0	V	a	r
10	i	a	b	l	e	\0	a	b	l	e
20	\0	\0	x	x	\0					

String Table Indexes

Index	String
0	*none*
1	name.
7	Variable
11	able
16	able
24	*null string*

Symbol Table

The symbol table of an object file holds information needed to locate and relocate a program's symbolic definitions and references. A symbol table index is a subscript into this array. Index 0 both designates the first entry in the table and serves as the undefined symbol index. The contents of an initial entry are specified in Table 2-17 on page 36.

Table 2-14 *Symbol Table First Entry*

Name	Value
STN_UNDEF	0

A symbol table entry has the format shown in Figure 2-3.

Figure 2-3
Symbol Table Entry Structure

```
typedef struct {
        Elf32_Word      st_name;
        Elf32_Addr      st_value;
        Elf32_Word      st_size;
        unsigned char   st_info;
        unsigned char   st_other;
        Elf32_Half      st_shndx;
} Elf32_Sym;
```

The members have the following meaning.

`st_name` Holds an index into the object file's symbol string table, which holds the character representations of the symbol names. If the value is non-zero, then it represents a string table index that gives the symbol name. Otherwise, the symbol table entry has no name. Note that external C symbols have the same names in C and object file symbol tables.

`st_value` Gives the value of the associated symbol. Depending on the context, the value can be an absolute value, an address, or so forth. Details are provided below.

`st_size` Holds 0 if the symbol has no size or an unknown size. Many symbols have associated sizes. For example, the size of a data object is the number of bytes contained in the object.

`st_info` Specifies the symbol binding (see page 33) and type (see page 34) attributes. The following code shows how to manipulate the values.

```
#define ELF32_ST_BIND(i)    ((i)>>4)
#define ELF32_ST_TYPE(i)    ((i)&0xf)
#define ELF32_ST_INFO(b,t)  (((b))<<4)+((t)&0xf))
```

`st_other` Currently, holds 0 and has no defined meaning.

`st_shndx` Every symbol table entry is *defined* in relation to some section. This member holds the relevant section header table index. Some section indexes indicate special meanings.

Symbol Binding

A symbol's binding determines the linkage visibility and behavior. Symbol binding values are listed in Table 2-15.

Table 2-15 *Symbol Binding, ELF32_ST_BIND*

Name	Value
STB_LOCAL	0
STB_GLOBAL	1
STB_WEAK	2
STB_LOPROC	13
STB_HIPROC	15

The bindings have the following meaning.

`STB_LOCAL`
: Local symbols are not visible outside the object file containing their definition. Local symbols of the same name can exist in multiple files without interfering with each other.

`STB_GLOBAL`
: Global symbols are visible to all object files being combined. One file's definition of a global symbol will satisfy another file's undefined reference to the same global symbol.

`STB_WEAK`
: Weak symbols resemble global symbols, but their definitions have lower precedence.

`STB_LOPROC` through `STB_HIPROC`
: Values in this inclusive range are reserved for processor-specific semantics.

Global and weak symbols differ in two major ways.

- ▲ When the link editor combines several relocatable object files, it does not allow multiple definitions of STB_GLOBAL symbols with the same name. On the other hand, if a defined global symbol exists, then the appearance of a weak symbol with the same name will not cause an error. The link editor honors the global definition and ignores the weak ones.

  Similarly, if a common symbol exists (for example, a symbol whose st_shndx field holds SHN_COMMON), the appearance of a weak symbol with the same name will not cause an error. The link editor honors the common definition and ignores the weak one.

- ▲ When the link editor searches archive libraries, it extracts archive members that contain definitions of undefined global symbols. The member definition can be either a global or a weak symbol. The link editor does not extract archive members to resolve undefined weak symbols. Unresolved weak symbols have a zero value.

In each symbol table, all symbols with STB_LOCAL binding precede the weak and global symbols. As described in "Section Header" on page 19, the sh_info section header member of a symbol table section holds the symbol table index for the first non-local symbol.

Symbol Types

A symbol type provides a general classification for the associated entity. Types are listed in Table 2-16.

Table 2-16 *Symbol Types, ELF32_ST_TYPE*

Name	Value
STT_NOTYPE	0
STT_OBJECT	1
STT_FUNC	2
STT_SECTION	3
STT_FILE	4
STT_LOPROC	13
STT_HIPROC	15

The types have the following meaning.

STT_NOTYPE
The symbol type is not specified.

STT_OBJECT
The symbol is associated with a data object, such as a variable, an array, and so forth.

STT_FUNC The symbol is associated with a function or other executable code.

STT_SECTION
The symbol is associated with a section. Symbol table entries of this type exist primarily for relocation and normally have STB_LOCAL binding.

STT_FILE Conventionally, the symbol name gives the name of the source file associated with the object file. A file symbol has STB_LOCAL binding, its section index is SHN_ABS, and it precedes the other STB_LOCAL symbols for the file, if it is present.

STT_LOPROC through STT_HIPROC
Reserved for processor-specific semantics.

Function symbols (those with type STT_FUNC) in shared object files have special significance. When another object file references a function from a shared object, the link editor automatically creates a procedure linkage table entry for the referenced symbol. Shared object symbols with types other than STT_FUNC will not be referenced automatically through the procedure linkage table.

If a symbol value refers to a specific location within a section, its section index member, st_shndx, holds an index into the section header table. As the section moves during relocation, the symbol value changes as well, and references to the symbol continue to "point" to the same location in the program. Some special section index values give other semantics:

SHN_ABS The symbol has an absolute value that will not change because of relocation.

SHN_COMMON

The symbol labels a common block that has not yet been allocated. The symbol's value gives alignment constraints, similar to a section's sh_addralign member. The link editor allocates the storage for the symbol at an address that is a multiple of st_value. The symbol size tells how many bytes are required.

SHN_UNDEF

This section table index means the symbol is undefined. When the link editor combines this object file with another that defines the indicated symbol, this file's references to the symbol will be linked to the actual definition.

The symbol table entry for index 0 (STN_UNDEF) is reserved and holds the values listed in Table 2-17.

Table 2-17 ***Symbol Table Entry: Index 0***

Name	Value	Note
st_name	0	No name
st_value	0	Zero value
st_size	0	No size
st_info	0	No type, local binding
st_other	0	
st_shndx	SHN_UNDEF	No section

Symbol Values

Symbol table entries for different object file types have slightly different interpretations for the st_value member.

- In relocatable files, st_value holds alignment constraints for a symbol whose section index is SHN_COMMON.
- In relocatable files, st_value holds a section offset for a defined symbol. st_value is an offset from the beginning of the section that st_shndx identifies.

▲ In executable and shared object files, `st_value` holds a virtual address. To make these files' symbols more useful for the dynamic linker, the section offset (file interpretation) gives way to a virtual address (memory interpretation) for which the section number is irrelevant.

Although the symbol table values have similar meanings for different object files, the data allow efficient access by the appropriate programs.

❑ Relocation

Relocation is the process of connecting symbolic references with symbolic definitions. For example, when a program calls a function, the associated call instruction must transfer control to the proper destination address at execution. In other words, relocatable files must have information that describes how to modify their section contents, thus allowing executable and shared object files to hold the correct information for the program image of a process. *Relocation entries* are these data.

Relocation entries are described in detail in the *System V Application Binary Interface* machine specific supplements.

Figure 2-4 *Relocation Entries Structure*

```
typedef struct {
        Elf32_Addr      r_offset;
        Elf32_Word      r_info;
} Elf32_Rel;

typedef struct {
        Elf32_Addr      r_offset;
        Elf32_Word      r_info;
        Elf32_Sword     r_addend;
} Elf32_Rela;
```

The members have the following meaning.

`r_offset` Specifies the location at which to apply the relocation action. For a relocatable file, the value is the byte offset from the beginning of the section to the storage unit affected by the relocation. For an executable file or a shared object, the value is the virtual address of the storage unit affected by the relocation.

`r_info` Specifies both the symbol table index with respect to which the relocation must be made and the type of relocation to apply. For example, a call instruction's relocation entry would hold the symbol table index of the function being called. If the index is `STN_UNDEF`, the undefined symbol index, then the relocation uses 0 as the *symbol value*.

Relocation types are processor-specific; descriptions of their behavior appear below. When the text below refers to a relocation entry's relocation type or symbol table index, it means the result of applying `ELF32_R_TYPE` or `ELF32_R_SYM`, respectively, to the entry's `r_info` member.

```
#define ELF32_R_SYM(i)     (i)>>8)
#define ELF32_R_TYPE(i)    ((unsigned char)(i))
#define ELF32_R_INFO(s,t) (((s)<<8)+(unsigned char)(t))
```

`r_addend` Specifies a constant addend used to compute the value to be stored into the relocatable field.

Only `Elf32_Rela` entries contain an explicit addend. Entries of type `Elf32_Rel` store an implicit addend in the location to be modified. Depending on the processor architecture, one form or the other might be necessary or more convenient. Consequently, an implementation for a particular machine might use one form exclusively or either form, depending on context.

A relocation section references two other sections: a symbol table and a section to modify. The section header `sh_info` and `sh_link` members specify these relationships. Relocation entries for different object files have slightly different interpretations for the `r_offset` member. (See "Section Header" on page 19 for more information.)

▲ In relocatable files, `r_offset` holds a section offset. The relocation section itself describes how to modify another section in the file; relocation offsets designate a storage unit within the second section.

- ▲ In executable and shared object files, `r_offset` holds a virtual address. To make the relocation entries of these files more useful for the dynamic linker, the section offset (file interpretation) gives way to a virtual address (memory interpretation).

Although the interpretation of `r_offset` changes for different object files to allow efficient access by the relevant programs, the meanings of the relocation types stay the same.

Relocation types are processor-specific. The ABI supplement for the specific processor describes the details.

3

Program Execution

The "execution" view of an object file, illustrated in Figure 1-2, includes the ELF header (described in Chapter 2), a program header table, segments, and the optional section header table (also described in Chapter 2). This chapter describes the "execution" entities. It also describes the object file information and system actions that create running programs. Some information here applies to all systems; information specific to one processor resides in sections marked accordingly.

Executable and shared object files statically represent programs. To execute such programs, the system uses the files to create dynamic program representations, or process images. A process image has segments that hold its text, data, stack, and so forth. The major sections of the chapter discuss the following subjects.

- ▲ Program header — The primary data structure, a program header table, locates segment images within the file and contains other information necessary to create a memory image for the program.
- ▲ Program loading — Given an object file, the system must load it into memory for the program to run.

▲ Dynamic linking — After the system loads the program, it must complete the process image by resolving symbolic references among the object files that compose the process.

The processor supplement defines a naming convention for ELF constants that have processor ranges specified. Names such as `DT_`, `PT_`, for processor specific extensions, incorporate the name of the processor: `DT_M32_SPECIAL`, for example. Pre-existing processor extensions, such as `DT_JMP_REL`, not using this convention will be supported.

❑ Program Header

The program header table of an executable or shared object file is an array of structures, each describing a segment or other information the system needs to prepare the program for execution. An object file segment contains one or more sections. (See "Segment Contents" on page 47 for more information.) Program headers are meaningful only for executable and shared object files. A file specifies its own program header size with the ELF header `e_phentsize` and `e_phnum` members. (See "ELF Header" on page 11 for more information.)

Figure 3-1 *Program Header Structure*

```
typedef struct {
        Elf32_Word      p_type;
        Elf32_Off       p_offset;
        Elf32_Addr      p_vaddr;
        Elf32_Addr      p_paddr;
        Elf32_Word      p_filesz;
        Elf32_Word      p_memsz;
        Elf32_Word      p_flags;
        Elf32_Word      p_align;
} Elf32_Phdr;
```

The members have the following meaning.

`p_type` Specifies what kind of segment this array element describes or how to interpret the array element's information. Type values and their meanings are described in "Segment Types (p_type)" on page 43.

`p_offset` Specifies the offset from the beginning of the file at which the first byte of the segment resides.

`p_vaddr` Specifies the virtual address at which the first byte of the segment resides in memory.

`p_paddr` On systems for which physical addressing is relevant, reserved for the segment's physical address. Because UNIX System V ignores physical addressing for application programs, this member has unspecified contents for executable files and shared objects.

`p_filesz` Specifies the number of bytes in the file image of the segment; it may be zero.

`p_memsz` Specifies the number of bytes in the memory image of the segment; it may be zero.

`p_flags` Specifies flags relevant to the segment. Defined flag values are listed in Table 3-2 on page 46.

`p_align` Loadable process segments must have congruent values for `p_vaddr` and `p_offset`, modulo the page size. (See "Program Loading (Processor-Specific)" on page 50 for more information.) This member gives the value to which the segments are aligned in memory and in the file. Values 0 and 1 mean no alignment is required. Otherwise, `p_align` should be a positive, integral power of 2, and `p_vaddr` should equal `p_offset`, modulo `p_align`.

Segment Types (`p_type`)

Some entries describe process segments; others give supplementary information and do not contribute to the process image. Unless specifically required elsewhere, all program header segment types are optional. The program header table of a file might contain only those elements relevant to its contents.

Segment entries can appear in any order, except as explicitly noted below. Defined type values are listed in Table 3-1; other values are reserved for future use.

Table 3-1 *Segment Types, p_type*

Name	Value
PT_NULL	0
PT_LOAD	1
PT_DYNAMIC	2
PT_INTERP	3
PT_NOTE	4
PT_SHLIB	5
PT_PHDR	6
PT_LOPROC	0x70000000
PT_HIPROC	0x7fffffff

The segment types have the following meaning.

PT_NULL Unused; values of other members are undefined. This type allows the program header table to contain ignored entries.

PT_LOAD Specifies a loadable segment, described by p_filesz and p_memsz. The bytes from the file are mapped to the beginning of the memory segment. If the segment memory size (p_memsz) is larger than the file size (p_filesz), the "extra" bytes are defined to hold the value 0 and to follow the segment's initialized area. The file size cannot be larger than the memory size. Loadable segment entries in the program header table appear in ascending order, sorted on the p_vaddr member.

PT_DYNAMIC

Specifies dynamic linking information. (See "Dynamic Section" on page 56 for more information.)

PT_INTERP
: Specifies the location and size of a null-terminated path name to invoke as an interpreter. This segment type is meaningful only for executable files (though it may occur for shared objects); it may not occur more than once in a file. If it is present, it must precede any loadable segment entry. (See "Program Interpreter" on page 54 for more information.)

PT_NOTE
: Specifies the location and size of auxiliary information. (See "Note Section" on page 48 for more information.)

PT_SHLIB
: This segment type is reserved but has unspecified semantics.

PT_PHDR
: If present, specifies the location and size of the program header table itself, both in the file and in the memory image of the program. This segment type may not occur more than once in a file. Moreover, it may occur only if the program header table is part of the memory image of the program. If it is present, it must precede any loadable segment entry. (See "Program Interpreter" on page 54 for more information.)

PT_LOPROC through PT_HIPROC
: Reserved for processor-specific semantics.

Base Address

The base address relocates the memory image of a program during dynamic linking. The virtual addresses in the program headers might not represent the actual virtual addresses of the program memory image. Executable files typically contain absolute code. For correct execution of the process, the segments must reside at the virtual addresses used to build the executable file. On the other hand, shared object segments typically contain position-independent code. This independence lets a segment's virtual address change from one process to another, without invalidating execution behavior.

Although the system chooses virtual addresses for individual processes, it maintains the segments' *relative positions*. Because position-independent code uses relative addressing between segments, the difference between virtual addresses in memory must match the difference between virtual addresses in the file. The difference between the virtual address of any segment in memory and the corresponding virtual address in the file is thus a single constant value for any one executable or shared object in a given process. This difference is the *base address*.

An executable or shared object file's base address is calculated during execution from three values: the memory load address, the maximum page size, and the lowest virtual address of a program's loadable segment. To compute the base address, you determine the memory address associated with the lowest `p_vaddr` value for a `PT_LOAD` segment. The address is truncated to the nearest multiple of the maximum page size. The corresponding `p_vaddr` value itself is also truncated to the nearest multiple of the maximum page size. The base address is the difference between the truncated memory address and the truncated `p_vaddr` value.

Segment Permissions

A program to be loaded by the system must have at least one loadable segment (although this is not required by the file format). When the system creates memory images of loadable segments, it gives access permissions as specified in the `p_flags` member, as listed in Table 3-2.

Table 3-2 *Segment Flag Bits,* **`p_flags`**

Name	Value	Meaning
PF_X	0x1	Execute
PF_W	0x2	Write
PF_R	0x4	Read
PF_MASKPROC	0xf0000000	Unspecified. All bits included in the mask are reserved for processor-specific semantics.

If a permission bit is 0, then that type of access is denied. Actual memory permissions depend on the memory management unit, which may vary from one system to another. Although all flag combinations are valid, the system may grant more access than requested. However, a segment will never have write permission unless it is specified explicitly. Table 3-3 lists both the exact flag interpretation and the allowable flag interpretation.

Table 3-3 *Segment Permissions*

Flags	Value	Exact	Allowable
none	0	All access denied	All access denied
PF_X	1	Execute only	Read, execute
PF_W	2	Write only	Read, write, execute
PF_W+PF_X	3	Write, execute	Read, write, execute
PF_R	4	Read only	Read, execute
PF_R+PF_X	5	Read, execute	Read, execute
PF_R+PF_W	6	Read, write	Read, write, execute
PF_R+PF_W+PF_X	7	Read, write, execute	Read, write, execute

For example, typical text segments have read and execute— but not write — permissions. Data segments normally have read, write, and execute permissions.

Segment Contents

An object file segment comprises one or more sections, though this fact is transparent to the program header. Whether the file segment holds one or many sections also is immaterial to program loading. Nonetheless, various data must be present for program execution, dynamic linking, and so on. Figure 3-2 illustrates segment contents in general terms. The order and membership of sections within a segment can vary; moreover, processor-specific constraints may alter the examples below. Other sections can also reside in loadable segments; these examples are not meant to give complete and exclusive segment contents.

Figure 3-2
Segment Contents

Text segments contain read-only instructions and data, typically as shown.

Data segments contain writable data and instructions, typically as shown.

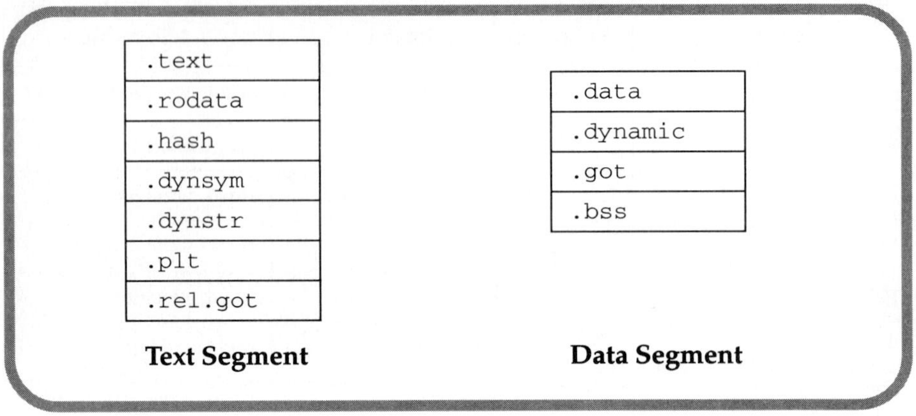

A `PT_DYNAMIC` program header element points at the `.dynamic` section. (See "Dynamic Section" on page 56 for more information.) The `.got` and `.plt` sections also hold information related to position-independent code and dynamic linking. Although the `.plt` appears in a text segment in the previous table, it may reside in a text or a data segment, depending on the processor. (See "Global Offset Table and Procedure Linkage Table" on page 64 and "Initialization and Termination Functions" on page 64 for more information.)

The `.bss` section has the type `SHT_NOBITS`. Although it occupies no space in the file, it contributes to the segment's memory image. Normally, these uninitialized data reside at the end of the segment, thereby making `p_memsz` larger than `p_filesz` in the associated program header element.

Note Section

Sometimes a vendor or system builder needs to mark an object file with special information that other programs will check for conformance, compatibility, and so forth. Sections of type `SHT_NOTE` and program header elements of type `PT_NOTE` can be used for this purpose. Labels help explain note information organization, but they are not part of the specification.

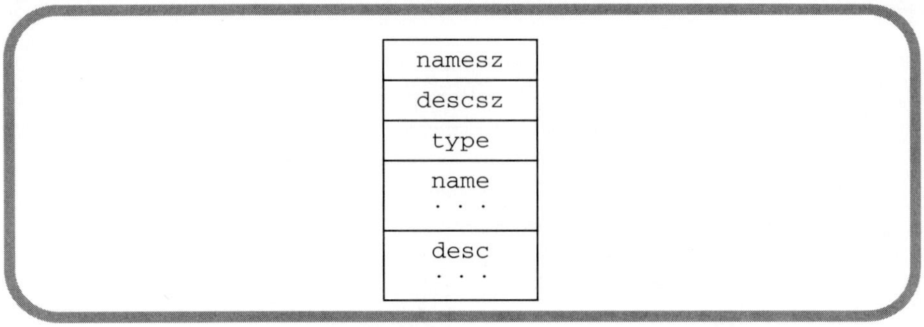

Figure 3-3
Note Information
The note information in sections and program header elements holds a variable number of entries, each of which is an array of 4-byte words in the format of the target processor.

The labels have the following meaning.

`namesz` and `name`
: The first `namesz` bytes in `name` contain a null-terminated character representation of the entry's owner or originator. There is no formal mechanism for avoiding name conflicts. By convention, vendors use their own name, such as **XYZ Computer Company**, as the identifier. If no name is present, then `namesz` contains 0. Padding is present, if necessary, to ensure 4-byte alignment for the descriptor. Such padding is not included in `namesz`.

  The system reserves note information with no name (`namesz==0`) and with a zero-length name (`name[0]=='\0'`) but currently defines no types. All other names must have at least one non-null character.

`descsz` and `desc`
: The first `descsz` bytes in `desc` hold the note descriptor. If no descriptor is present, then `descsz` contains 0. Padding is present, if necessary, to ensure 4-byte alignment for the next note entry. Such padding is not included in `descsz`.

`type`
: This word provides the interpretation of the descriptor. Each originator controls its own types; multiple interpretations of a single type value may exist. Thus, a program must recognize both the name and the type to recognize a descriptor. Currently, types must be non-negative.

To illustrate, the note segment shown in Figure 3-4 holds two entries.

Figure 3-4
Example Note Segment

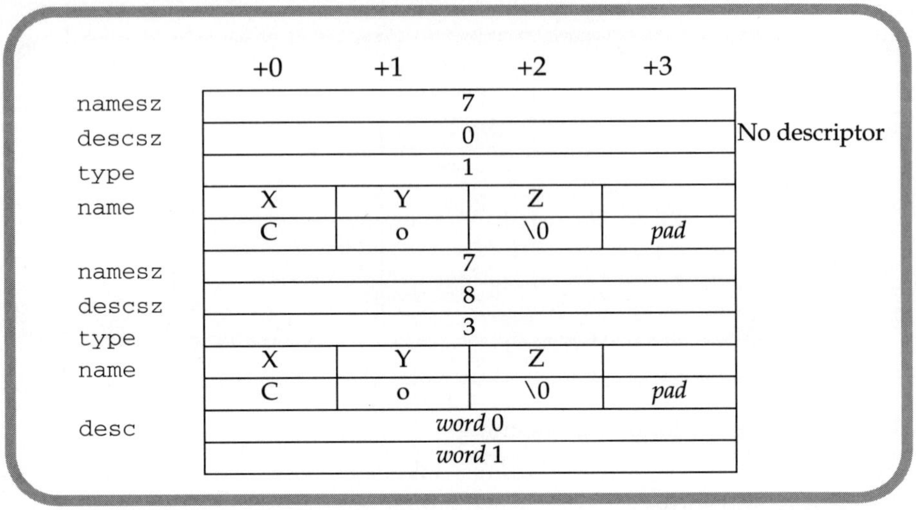

❑ Program Loading (Processor-Specific)

As the system creates or augments a process image, it logically copies a file's segment to a virtual memory segment. When—and if—the system physically reads the file depends on the program's execution behavior, system load, and so forth. A process does not require a physical page unless it references the logical page during execution, and processes commonly leave many pages unreferenced. Therefore, delaying physical reads frequently obviates them, improving system performance. To obtain this efficiency in practice, executable and shared object files must have segment images whose file offsets and virtual addresses are congruent, modulo the page size. By alignment of segments to the maximum page size, the files will be suitable for paging regardless of physical page size.

The following examples show 8 K alignment; virtual addresses and file offsets for segments are congruent modulo 8 K (`0x2000`). Actual minimum page sizes are machine specific.

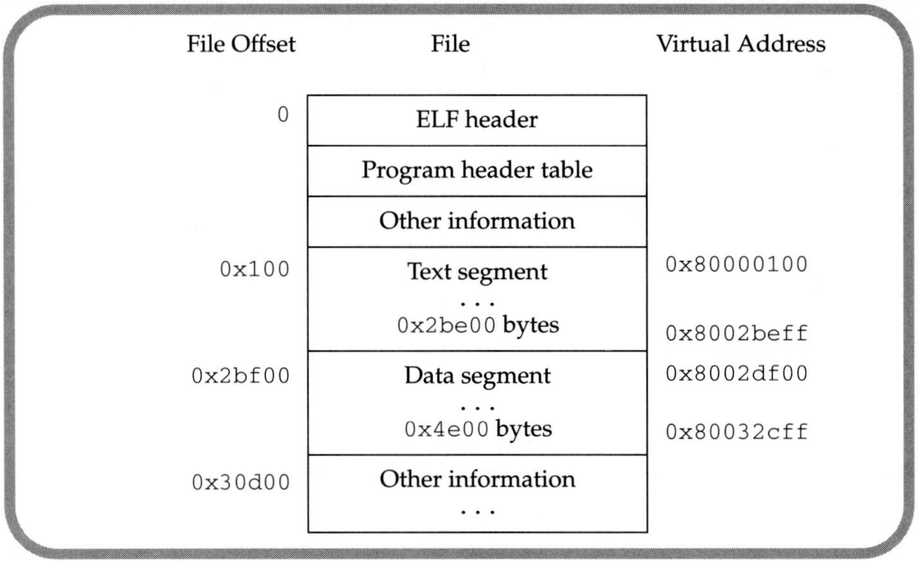

Figure 3-5
Executable File Example

Figure 3-6
Program Header Segments
Although the file offsets and virtual addresses are congruent modulo the maximum page size for both text and data, up to four file pages hold impure text or data (depending on page size and file system block size).

Member	Text	Data
p_type	PT_LOAD	PT_LOAD
p_offset	0x100	0x2bf00
p_vaddr	0x80000100	0x8002df00
p_paddr	unspecified	unspecified
p_filesz	0x2be00	0x4e00
p_memsz	0x2be00	0x5e24
p_flags	PF_R+PF_X	PF_R+PF_W+PF_X
p_align	0x2000	0x2000

- The first text page contains the ELF header, the program header table, and other information.
- The last text page holds a copy of the beginning of data.
- The first data page has a copy of the end of text.
- The last data page may contain file information not relevant to the running process.

Logically, the system enforces the memory permissions as if each segment were complete and separate; segments' addresses are adjusted to ensure that each logical page in the address space has a single set of permissions. In the previous example, the region of the file holding the end of text and the beginning of data will be mapped twice: at one virtual address for text and at a different virtual address for data.

The end of the data segment requires special handling for uninitialized data, which the system defines to begin with zero values. Thus, if a file's last data page includes information not in the logical memory page, then the extraneous data must be set to zero, not to the unknown contents of the executable file. *Impurities* in the other three pages are not logically part of the process image; whether the system expunges them is unspecified. The memory image for the program follows, assuming 2 KB (`0x800`) pages. For simplicity, the example illustrates only one page size.

Figure 3-7
Process Image Segments
The memory image assumes 2 KB (`0x800`) pages. For simplicity, only one page size is illustrated.

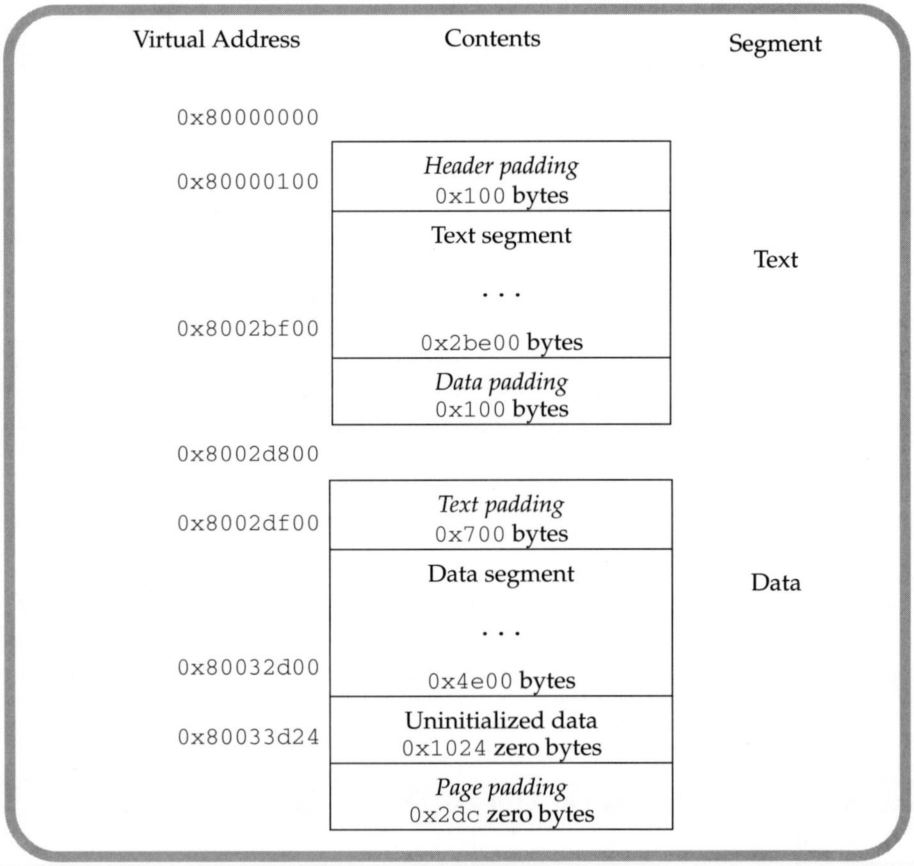

One aspect of segment loading differs between executable files and shared objects. Executable file segments typically contain absolute code. For the process to execute correctly, the segments must reside at the virtual addresses used to build the executable file. Thus, the system uses the `p_vaddr` values unchanged as virtual addresses.

On the other hand, shared object segments typically contain position-independent code. This independence lets a segment's virtual address change from one process to another, without invalidating execution behavior. Though the system chooses virtual addresses for individual processes, it maintains the segments' relative positions. Because position-independent code uses relative addressing between segments, the difference between virtual addresses in memory must match the difference between virtual addresses in the file.

Figure 3-8 presents possible shared object virtual address assignments for several processes, illustrating constant relative positioning

Figure 3-8 ***Example Shared Object Segment Addresses***
Base address computations are also illustrated. Maximum page size is 8KB.

Source	Text	Data	Base Address
File	0x200	0x2a400	0x0
Process 1	0xc0080200	0xc00aa400	0xc0080000
Process 2	0xc0082200	0xc00ac400	0xc0082000
Process 3	0xd00c0200	0xd00ea400	0xd00c0000
Process 4	0xd00c6200	0xd00f0400	0xd00c6000

❑ Dynamic Linking

Under dynamic linking, the contents of a shared object are mapped into the virtual address space of a process at runtime. External references in the program are connected with their definitions when the program is executed.

Program Interpreter

An executable file that participates in dynamic linking shall have one PT_INTERP program header element. During exec(2), the system retrieves a path name from the PT_INTERP segment and creates the initial process image from the interpreter file's segments. Instead of using the original executable file's segment images, the system composes a memory image for the interpreter. It is then the interpreter's responsibility to receive control from the system and provide an environment for the application program.

The interpreter receives control in one of two ways. First, it may receive a file descriptor to read the executable file, positioned at the beginning. It can use this file descriptor to read and/or map the executable file's segments into memory. Second, depending on the executable file format, the system may load the executable file into memory instead of giving the interpreter an open file descriptor. With the possible exception of the file descriptor, the interpreter's initial process state matches what the executable file would have received. The interpreter itself might not require a second interpreter. An interpreter can be either a shared object or an executable file.

- A shared object (the normal case) is loaded as position-independent, with addresses that may vary from one process to another; the system creates its segments in the dynamic segment area used by mmap(2) and related services. Consequently, a shared object interpreter typically will not conflict with the original segment addresses of the original executable file.
- An executable file is loaded at fixed addresses; the system creates its segments by using the virtual addresses from the program header table. Consequently, an executable file interpreter's virtual addresses may collide with the first executable file; the interpreter is responsible for resolving conflicts.

Dynamic Linker

When building an executable file that uses dynamic linking, the link editor adds a program header element of type PT_INTERP to an executable file, instructing the system to invoke the dynamic linker as the program interpreter. (The locations of the system-provided dynamic linkers are processor-specific.) exec(2) and the dynamic linker cooperate to create the process image for the program, which entails the following actions:

1. Adding the executable file's memory segments to the process image.
2. Adding shared object memory segments to the process image.
3. Performing relocations for the executable file and its shared objects.
4. Closing the file descriptor that was used to read the executable file, if one was given to the dynamic linker.
5. Transferring control to the program, making it look as if the program had received control directly from `exec`(2).

The link editor also constructs various data that assist the dynamic linker for executable and shared object files. These data reside in loadable segments, making them available during execution. (Again, recall that the exact segment contents are processor-specific. See the processor supplement for complete information.)

- A `.dynamic` section with type `SHT_DYNAMIC` holds various data. The structure residing at the beginning of the section holds the addresses of other dynamic linking information.
- The `.hash` section with type `SHT_HASH` holds a symbol hash table.
- The `.got` and `.plt` sections with type `SHT_PROGBITS` hold two separate tables: the global offset table and the procedure linkage table. Sections below explain how the dynamic linker uses and changes the tables to create memory images for object files.

Shared objects can occupy virtual memory addresses that are different from the addresses recorded in the file's program header table. The dynamic linker relocates the memory image, updating absolute addresses before the application gains control. Although the absolute address values would be correct if the library were loaded at the addresses specified in the program header table, that case is not the norm.

If the process environment contains a variable named with a non-null value, then the dynamic linker processes all relocations before transferring control to the program. For example, all the following environment entries would specify this behavior.

- `LD_BIND_NOW=1`
- `LD_BIND_NOW=on`
- `LD_BIND_NOW=off`

Otherwise, LD_BIND_NOW either does not occur in the environment or has a null value. The dynamic linker is permitted to evaluate procedure linkage table entries slowly, thus avoiding symbol resolution and relocation overhead for functions that are not called.

Dynamic Section

If an object file participates in dynamic linking, then its program header table will have an element of type PT_DYNAMIC. This *segment* contains the .dynamic section. A special symbol, _DYNAMIC, labels the section, which contains an array of the following structures.

Figure 3-9
_Dynamic Structure

```
typedef struct {
        Elf32_Sword  d_tag;
        union {
              Elf32_Word      d_val;
              Elf32_Addr      d_ptr;
        } d_un;
} Elf32_Dyn;

extern Elf32_Dyn     _DYNAMIC[];
```

For each object with this type, d_tag controls the interpretation of d_un.

d_val — These Elf32_Word objects represent integer values with various interpretations.

d_ptr — These Elf32_Addr objects represent program virtual addresses; a file's virtual addresses might not match the memory virtual addresses during execution. When interpreting addresses contained in the dynamic structure, the dynamic linker computes actual addresses, based on the original file value and the memory base address. For consistency, files do *not* contain relocation entries to *correct* addresses in the dynamic structure.

Table 3-4 summarizes the tag requirements for executable and shared object files. If a tag is marked *mandatory,* then the dynamic linking array must have an entry of that type. Likewise, *optional* means an entry for the tag may appear but is not required.

Table 3-4 *Dynamic Array Tags, `d_tag`*

Name	Value	d_un	Executable	Shared Object
DT_NULL	0	ignored	mandatory	mandatory
DT_NEEDED	1	d_val	optional	optional
DT_PLTRELSZ	2	d_val	optional	optional
DT_PLTGOT	3	d_ptr	optional	optional
DT_HASH	4	d_ptr	mandatory	mandatory
DT_STRTAB	5	d_ptr	mandatory	mandatory
DT_SYMTAB	6	d_ptr	mandatory	mandatory
DT_RELA	7	d_ptr	mandatory	optional
DT_RELASZ	8	d_val	mandatory	optional
DT_RELAENT	9	d_val	mandatory	optional
DT_STRSZ	10	d_val	mandatory	mandatory
DT_SYMENT	11	d_val	mandatory	mandatory
DT_INIT	12	d_ptr	optional	optional
DT_FINI	13	d_ptr	optional	optional
DT_SONAME	14	d_val	ignored	optional
DT_RPATH	15	d_val	optional	ignored
DT_SYMBOLIC	16	ignored	ignored	optional
DT_REL	17	d_ptr	mandatory	optional
DT_RELSZ	18	d_val	mandatory	optional
DT_RELENT	19	d_val	mandatory	optional
DT_PLTREL	20	d_val	optional	optional
DT_DEBUG	21	d_ptr	optional	ignored
DT_TEXTREL	22	ignored	optional	optional
DT_JMPREL	23	d_ptr	optional	optional
DT_LOPROC	0x70000000	unspecified	unspecified	unspecified
DT_HIPROC	0x7fffffff	unspecified	unspecified	unspecified

The elements have the following meaning.

DT_NULL An entry with a DT_NULL tag marks the end of the _DYNAMIC array.

DT_NEEDED
Holds the string table offset of a null-terminated string, specifying the name of a needed library. The offset is an index into the table recorded in the DT_STRTAB entry. (See "Shared Object Dependencies" on page 61 for more information about the names.) The dynamic array may contain multiple entries with this type. The relative order of these entries is significant, though their relation to entries of other types is not.

DT_PLTRELSZ
Holds the total size, in bytes, of the relocation entries associated with the procedure linkage table. If an entry of type DT_JMPREL is present, then a DT_PLTRELSZ must accompany it.

DT_PLTGOT
Holds an address associated with the procedure linkage table and/or the global offset table. Semantics are processor specific.

DT_HASH Holds the address of the symbol hash table, described in "Hash Table" on page 63.

DT_STRTAB
Holds the address of the string table, described "String Table" on page 30. Symbol names, library names, and other strings reside in this table.

DT_SYMTAB
Holds the address of the symbol table, described in "Symbol Table" on page 31, with Elf32_Sym entries for the 32-bit class of files.

DT_RELA Holds the address of a relocation table, described in "Relocation" on page 37. Entries in the table have explicit addends, such as Elf32_Rela for the 32-bit file class. An object file may have multiple relocation sections. When relocation is "mandatory" for a file, either DT_RELA or DT_REL can occur; both are permitted but not required.

When building the relocation table for an executable or shared object file, the link editor catenates those sections to form a single table. Although the sections remain independent in the object file, the dynamic linker sees a single table.

When the dynamic linker creates the process image for an executable file or adds a shared object to the process image, it reads the relocation table and performs the associated actions. If this element is present, the dynamic structure must also have DT_RELASZ and DT_RELAENT elements.

DT_RELASZ
: Holds the total size, in bytes, of the DT_RELA relocation table.

DT_RELAENT
: Holds the size, in bytes, of the DT_RELA relocation entry.

DT_STRSZ
: Holds the size, in bytes, of the string table.

DT_SYMENT
: Holds the size, in bytes, of a symbol table entry.

DT_INIT
: Holds the address of the initialization function. (See "Initialization and Termination Functions" on page 64 for more information.)

DT_FINI
: Holds the address of the termination function. (See "Initialization and Termination Functions" on page 64 for more information.)

DT_SONAME
: Holds the string table offset of a null-terminated string, giving the name of the shared object. The offset is an index into the table recorded in the DT_STRTAB entry. (See "Shared Object Dependencies" on page 61 for more information about these names.)

`DT_RPATH` Holds the string table offset of a null-terminated search library search path string. The offset is an index into the table recorded in the `DT_STRTAB` entry.

`DT_SYMBOLIC`
This element's presence in a shared object library alters the dynamic linker's symbol resolution algorithm for references within the library. Instead of starting a symbol search with the executable file, the dynamic linker starts from the shared object itself. If the shared object fails to supply the referenced symbol, then the dynamic linker searches the executable file and other shared objects as usual.

`DT_REL` Similar to `DT_RELA`, except that its table has implicit addends, such as `Elf32_Rel` for the 32-bit file class. If this element is present, the dynamic structure must also have `DT_RELSZ` and `DT_RELENT` elements.

`DT_RELSZ` Holds the total size, in bytes, of the `DT_REL` relocation table.

`DT_RELENT`
Holds the size, in bytes, of the `DT_REL` relocation entry.

`DT_PLTREL`
Specifies the type of relocation entry to which the procedure linkage table refers. The `d_val` member holds `DT_REL` or `DT_RELA`, as appropriate. All relocations in a procedure linkage table must use the same relocation.

`DT_DEBUG` Used for debugging.

`DT_TEXTREL`
This member's absence signifies that no relocation entry should cause a modification to a non-writable segment, as specified by the segment permissions in the program header table. If this member is present, one or more relocation entries might request modifications to a non-writable segment, and the dynamic linker can prepare accordingly.

DT_JMPREL

If present, this entry's d_ptr member holds the address of relocation entries associated solely with the procedure linkage table. Separating these relocation entries lets the dynamic linker ignore them during process initialization, if lazy binding is enabled. If this entry is present, the related entries of types DT_PLTRELSZ and DT_PLTREL must also be present.

DT_LOPROC through DT_HIPROC

Reserved for processor-specific semantics.

Except for the DT_NULL element at the end of the array and the relative order of DT_NEEDED elements, entries may appear in any order. Tag values not appearing in the table are reserved.

Shared Object Dependencies

When the link editor processes an archive library, it extracts library members and copies them into the output object file. These statically linked services are available during execution without involving the dynamic linker. Shared objects also provide services, and the dynamic linker must attach the proper shared object files to the process image for execution. Thus, executable and shared object files describe their specific dependencies.

When the dynamic linker creates the memory segments for an object file, the dependencies (recorded in DT_NEEDED entries of the dynamic structure) tell what shared objects are needed to supply the program's services. By repeatedly connecting referenced shared objects and their dependencies, the dynamic linker builds a complete process image. When resolving symbolic references, the dynamic linker examines the symbol tables with a breadth-first search. It first looks at the symbol table of the executable program itself, then at the symbol tables of the DT_NEEDED entries (in order), and then at the second level DT_NEEDED entries, and so forth. Shared object files must be readable by the process; other permissions are not required.

Even when a shared object is referenced multiple times in the dependency list, the dynamic linker connects the object only once to the process.

Names in the dependency list are copies either of the `DT_SONAME` strings or the path names of the shared objects used to build the object file. For example, if the link editor builds an executable file using one shared object with a `DT_SONAME` entry of `lib1` and another shared object library with the path name `/usr/lib/lib2`, then the executable file contains `lib1` and `/usr/lib/lib2` in its dependency list.

If a shared object name has one or more slash (`/`) characters anywhere in the name, such as `/usr/lib/lib2` or `directory/file`, then the dynamic linker uses that string directly as the path name. If the name has no slashes, such as `lib1`, then three facilities specify shared object path searching, with the following precedence:

1. The dynamic array tag `DT_RPATH` may give a string that holds a list of directories, separated by colons (`:`). For example, the string `/home/dir/usr/lib:/home/dir2/usr/lib:` tells the dynamic linker to search first the directory `/home/dir/lib`, then seacrch`/home/dir2/usr/lib`, and then search the current directory to find dependencies.
2. A variable called `LD_LIBRARY_PATH` in the process environment may hold a list of directories as above, optionally followed by a semicolon (`;`) and another directory list. The following values would be equivalent to the previous example:
   - `LD_LIBRARY_PATH=/home/dir/usr/lib:/home/dir2/usr/lib:`
   - `LD_LIBRARY_PATH=/home/dir/usr/lib;/home/dir2/usr/lib:`
   - `LD_LIBRARY_PATH=/home/dir/usr/lib:/home/dir2/usr/lib:;`

   All `LD_LIBRARY_PATH` directories are searched after those from `DT_RPATH`. Although some programs (such as the link editor) treat the lists before and after the semicolon differently, the dynamic linker does not. Nevertheless, the dynamic linker accepts the semicolon notation, with the semantics described previously.
3. If the other two groups of directories fail to locate the desired library, the dynamic linker searches `/usr/lib`.

For security, the dynamic linker ignores environmental search specifications (such as `LD_LIBRARY_PATH`) for set-user and set-group ID programs. It does, however, search `DT_RPATH` directories and `/usr/lib`.

Hash Table

A hash table of `Elf32_Word` objects supports symbol table access, as illustrated in Figure 3-10.

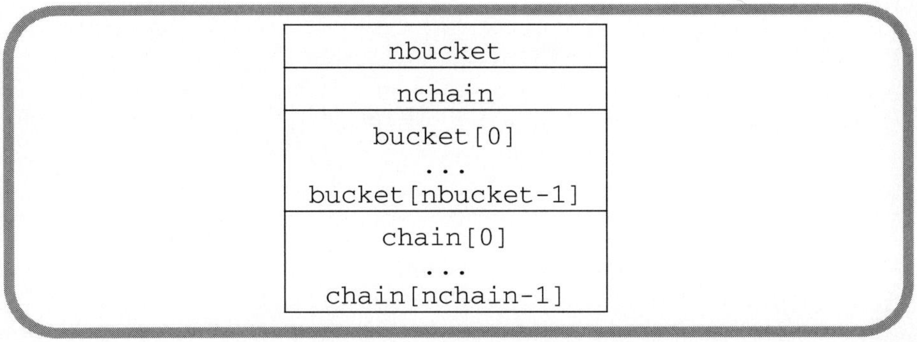

Figure 3-10
Symbol Hash Table
Labels are listed to help explain the hash table organization, but they are not part of the specification.

The `bucket` array contains `nbucket` entries, and the `chain` array contains `nchain` entries; indexes start at 0. Both `bucket` and `chain` hold symbol table indexes. Chain table entries parallel the symbol table. The number of symbol table entries should equal `nchain`; so symbol table indexes also select chain table entries.

A hashing function, shown in Figure 3-11, accepts a symbol name and returns a value that can be used to compute a `bucket` index. Consequently, if the hashing function returns the value *x* for some name, `bucket[`*x*`%nbucket]` gives an index, *y*, into both the symbol table and the chain table. If the symbol table entry is not the one desired, then `chain[`*y*`]` gives the next symbol table entry with the same hash value.

You can follow the `chain` links until either the selected symbol table entry holds the desired name or the `chain` entry contains the value `STN_UNDEF`.

Figure 3-11
Hashing Function

```
unsigned long
elf_hash(const unsigned char *name)
{
        unsigned longh = 0, g;

        while (*name)
        {
                        h = (h << 4) + *name++;
                        if (g = h & 0xf0000000)
                                h ^= g >> 24;
                        h &=  g;
        }
        return h;
}
```

Global Offset Table and Procedure Linkage Table

This section requires processor-specific information. The *System V Application Binary Interface* supplement for the desired processor describes the details of the global offset table and the procedure linkage table.

Initialization and Termination Functions

After the dynamic linker has built the process image and performed the relocations, each shared object has the opportunity to execute some initialization code. These initialization functions are called in no specified order, but all shared object initialization occurs before the executable file gains control.

Similarly, shared objects can have termination functions, which are executed with the `atexit`(3C) mechanism after the base process begins its termination sequence. Once again, the order in which the dynamic linker calls termination functions is unspecified.

Shared objects designate their initialization and termination functions through the `DT_INIT` and `DT_FINI` entries in the dynamic structure. (See "Dynamic Section" on page 56 for more information.) Typically, the code for these functions resides in the .init and .fini sections. (See "Section Header" in Chapter 2 for more information.)

Although the atexit(3C) termination processing normally is done, it is not guaranteed to have executed upon process death. In particular, the process will not execute the termination processing if it calls _exit() or if the process dies because it received a signal that it neither caught nor ignored.

Dynamic Linking Programming Interface

You can use a programming interface to the dynamic linking mechanism to attach a shared object to the address space of a process during execution, look up the address of a function in the library, call that function, and then detach the library when it is no longer needed. The routines for this procedure are stored in libdl.so.

When you use a shared library function, the entire contents of the library are mapped into the virtual address space of your process at runtime. External references to the function are assigned virtual addresses when the program is executed. The link editor records in the executable only the name of the shared object and a small amount of bookkeeping information for use by the dynamic linker.

Each process that uses a shared object references a single copy of its code in memory. Thus, when other users on a system call a function in a shared object library, the entire contents of that library are mapped into the virtual address space of their processes as well. If they have called the same function as you, external references to the function in their programs will be assigned, in all likelihood, different virtual addresses. Because the function may be loaded at a different virtual address for each process that uses it, the system cannot calculate absolute addresses in memory until runtime.

The memory management scheme underlying dynamic linking shares memory among processes at the granularity of a page. Memory pages can be shared as long as they are not modified at runtime. If a process writes to a shared page while relocating a reference to a shared object, then it receives a private copy of that page and loses the benefits of code sharing without affecting other users of the page.

To create programs that require the least possible amount of page modification at runtime, the compiler generates position-independent code under the `-K PIC` option, which causes code generation to be position-independent. Whereas executable code normally must be tied to a fixed address in memory, position-independent code can be loaded anywhere in the address space of a process. Because the code is not tied to specific addresses, it executes correctly — without page modification — at a different address in each process that uses it. Specify `-K PIC` when you create a shared object:

```
$ cc -K PIC -G -o libfoo.so function1.c function2.c \
    function3.c
```

Relocatable references in your object code will be moved from its text segment to tables in the data segment.

Dynamic Linking Facilities

A family of routines provides direct access to the dynamic linking facilities.

- `dlopen` — Opens a shared object
- `dlsym` — Obtains the address of a symbol in a shared object
- `dlerror` — Reports diagnostic information
- `dlclose` — Closes a shared object

The routines are available in a library that you load when you specify the option `-ldl` with the `cc` or `ld` command.

The `dlopen` Facility

```
cc [flag ...] file ... -ldl [library ...]
#include <dlfcn.h>
void *dlopen(const char *pathname, int mode);
```

`dlopen` makes a shared object available to a running process by returning to the process a handle which the process uses on subsequent calls to `dlsym` and `dlclose`. The process may not interpret the returned value in any way.

pathname specifies the path name of the object to be opened. It can be an absolute path or relative to the current directory. If the value of *pathname* is 0, then `dlopen` makes available through `dlsym` the symbols contained in the original `a.out`, as well as all the objects that `a.out` loaded at program startup. If *pathname* cannot be found, cannot be opened for reading, is not a shared object, or if an error occurs while *pathname* is being loaded or while its symbolic references are being relocated, then `dlopen` returns `NULL`.

When a shared object is brought into the address space of a process, it can contain references to symbols whose addresses are not known until the object is loaded. The references must be relocated before the symbols can be accessed. The value of *mode* determines when such relocation shall occur.

- ▲ To relocate only references to data symbols when an object is loaded, specify `RTLD_LAZY` for *mode*. References to functions are not relocated until a given function is invoked for the first time. Specifying `RTLD_LAZY` may result in better performance because a process may not reference all of the functions in any given shared object.
- ▲ To relocate all necessary functions when an object is first loaded, specify `RTLD_NOW` for *mode*. While some wasted effort may result if relocations are performed for functions that are never referenced, `RTLD_NOW` is useful when applications must know as soon as an object is loaded that all symbols referenced during execution will be made available.

See Figure 3-12 for an example of how to use `dlopen`.

The `dlsym` Facility

```
cc [flag ...] file ... -ldl [library ...]
#include <dlfcn.h>
void *dlsym(void *handle, const char *name);
```

`dlsym` allows a process to obtain the address of a symbol defined within a shared object previously opened by `dlopen`. `dlsym` searches for the symbol, specified as a character string by *name*, in all shared objects loaded automatically as a result of loading the object referred to by *handle* (returned by a call to `dlopen`).

If *handle* does not refer to a valid object opened by `dlopen` or if the named symbol cannot be found within any of the objects associated with *handle*, then `dlsym` returns `NULL`.

You can use `dlopen` and `dlsym` to access either function or data objects, as illustrated in Figure 3-12.

Figure 3-12
Example of Using dlopen and dlsym
For simplicity, error checking has been omitted.

```
void *handle;
int i, *iptr;
int (f*fptr)(int);

/* open the needed object */
handle - dlopen("/usr/mydir/libx.so", RTLD_LAZY

/* find address of function and data objects */
fptr = (int (*)(int))dlsym(handle, "some_functions");

iptr = (int *)dlsym(handle, "int_object");

/* invoke function, passing value of integer as a
parameter */

i = (*fptr)(*iptr);
```

The `dlerror` Facility

```
cc [flag ...] file ... -ldl [library ...]
#include <dlfcn.h>
char *dlerror(void);
```

`dlerror` provides detailed diagnostic information about errors that occurred during dynamic linking processing. The messages returned by `dlerror` may reside in a static buffer that is overwritten on each call to `dlerror`. Application code should not write to that buffer. Programs wishing to preserve an error message should make their own copies of that message.

If no errors occurred since the last invocation of `dlerror`, then `NULL` is returned. Thus, invoking `dlerror` a second time immediately following a prior invocation results in `NULL` being returned.

The `dlclose` Facility

```
cc [flag ...] file ... -ldl [library ...]
#include &lt;dlfcn.h&gt;
int dlclose(void *handle);
```

`dlclose` disassociates from the current process a shared object previously opened by `dlopen`. Once the object has thus been closed, its symbols are no longer available to `dlsym`, and referencing those symbols can cause undefined behavior. All objects loaded automatically as a result of the invocation of `dlopen` on the referenced object are also closed.

If the referenced object was successfully closed, then `dlclose` returns 0. A successful invocation of `dlclose` does not guarantee that the objects associated with *handle* (see `dlopen`) have actually been removed from the address space of the process. Objects loaded by one invocation of `dlopen` can also be loaded by another invocation of `dlopen`, and the same object can be opened multiple times. An object is not removed from the address space until all references to that object through an explicit `dlopen` invocation have been closed and all other objects implicitly referencing that object have also been closed.

If the object could not be closed or if *handle* does not refer to an open object, then `dlclose` returns a non-0 value. `dlerror` provides more detailed diagnostic information.

4

ELF Library Functions

Functions in the ELF access library allow a program to manipulate ELF object files, archive files, and archive members. The header file provides type and function declarations for all library services.

After an overview of ELF library constructs, conventions, and general use, this chapter explains the individual ELF functions contained in the ELF library.

❑ ELF Library Overview

The ELF library, `libelf.h`, is not implemented as a shared object and is not automatically linked by the C compilation system. To link with the library, specify `-lelf` on the `cc` command line. Figure 4-1 illustrates the ELF library contents.

Figure 4-1
ELF Library at a Glance

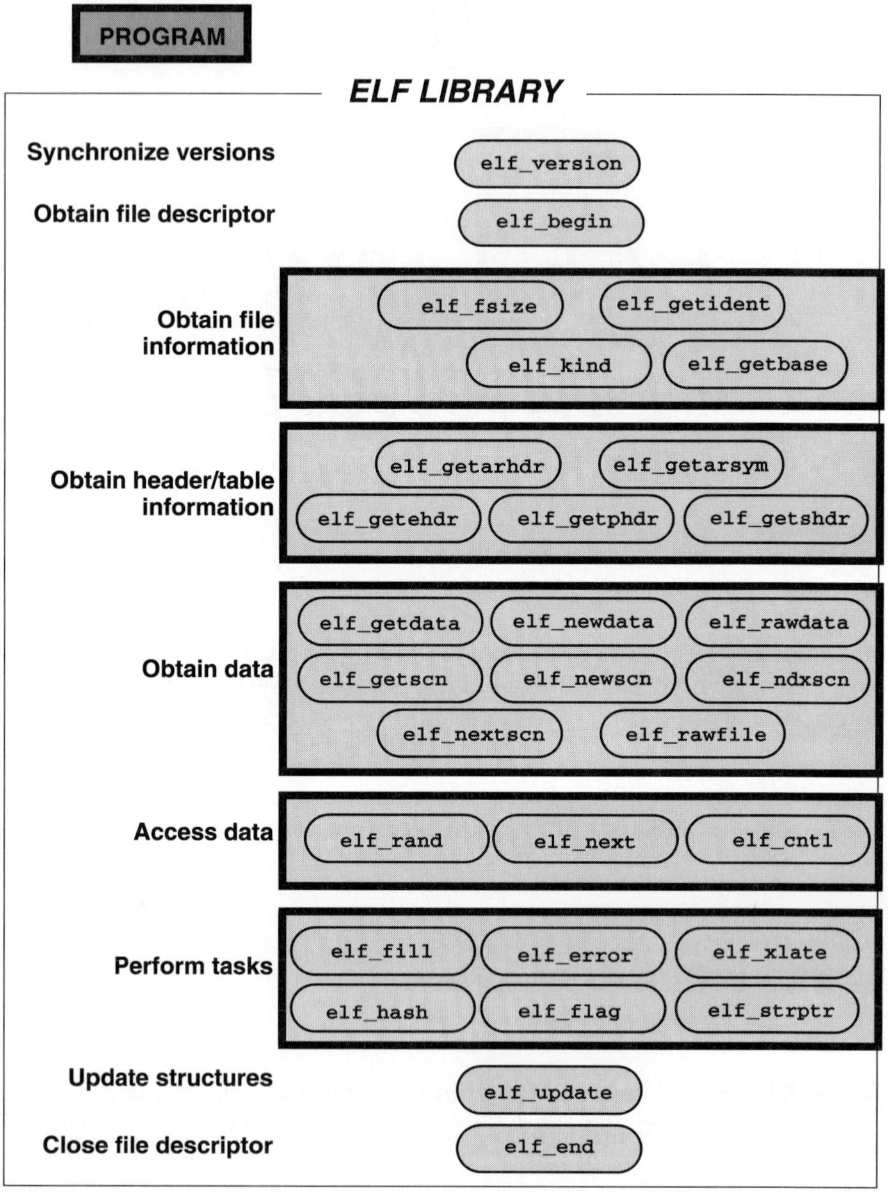

Descriptors

Descriptors provide private handles to a file and its pieces. In other words, a data descriptor is associated with one section descriptor, which is associated with one ELF descriptor, which is associated with one file. Although descriptors are private, they provide access to data that can be shared. Consider programs that combine input files, using incoming data to create or update another file. Such a program might get data descriptors for an input and an output section. It then could update the output descriptor to reuse the input descriptor's data. That is, the descriptors are distinct, but they could share the associated data bytes. This sharing avoids the space overhead for duplicate buffers and the performance overhead for copying data unnecessarily.

Programs communicate with many of the higher-level routines by means of an ELF descriptor. When a program starts working with a file, the ELF library function, `elf_begin` creates an ELF descriptor through which the program manipulates the structures and information in the file. ELF descriptors can be used both to read and to write files. If a program wishes to write data associated with the ELF descriptor to the file, then it uses `elf_update`. A program uses `elf_end` to terminate an ELF descriptor and to deallocate data associated with the descriptor.

After the program establishes an ELF descriptor for an object file, it may then obtain section descriptors to manipulate the sections of the file. Sections hold the bulk of an object file's real information, such as text, data, the symbol table, and so on. A section descriptor "belongs" to a particular ELF descriptor, just as a section belongs to a file.

Data descriptors, available through section descriptors, allow the program to manipulate the information associated with a section. A data descriptor "belongs" to a section descriptor.

ELF Versions

Object file versions allow ELF to adapt to new requirements. Three versions, which are independent, can be important to a program.

1. An application program knows about a particular version by virtue of being compiled with certain header files.

2. The access library similarly is compiled with header files that control what versions it understands.
3. An ELF object file holds a value identifying its version, determined by the ELF version known by the file's creator.

Ideally, all three versions would be the same, but they may differ, as follows.

- ▲ If a program's version is newer than the access library, then the program might use information unknown to the library. Translation routines might not work properly, leading to undefined behavior. This condition warrants installation of a new library.
- ▲ The library's version might be newer than the program and the file versions. The library understands old versions, thus avoiding compatibility problems.
- ▲ A file version might be newer than either the program or the library understands. The program might or might not be able to process the file properly, depending on whether the file has extra information and whether that information can safely be ignored. Again, the safe alternative is to install a new library that understands the file's version.

To accommodate the differences, a program must use `elf_version` to pass its version to the library, thus establishing the working version for the process. Using this version, the library accepts data from and presents data to the program in the proper representations. When the library reads object files, it uses each file's version to interpret the data. When writing files or converting memory types to the file equivalents, the library uses the program's working version for the data file.

Data Translation

Translation facilities convert between file and memory representation. Some library routines convert data automatically, while others leave conversion as the responsibility of the program. Either way, programs that create object files must write file-typed objects to those files; programs that read object files must take a similar view. (See `elf_xlate` on page 111 and `elf_fsize` on page 90 for more information.)

Programs may translate data explicitly, taking full control over the object file layout and semantics. If the program prefers not to have and exercise complete control, then the library provides a higher-level interface that hides many object file details. `elf_begin` and related functions let a program deal with the native memory types, converting between memory objects and their file equivalents automatically when reading or writing an object file.

Data Alignment

Data buffers within a section have explicit alignment constraints. Consequently, adjacent buffers sometimes will not abut, causing "holes" within a section. Programs that create output files have two ways of dealing with such holes.

- The program can use `elf_fill` to tell the library how to set the intervening bytes. When the library must generate gaps in the file, it uses the fill byte to initialize the data there. The library's initial fill value is zero, and `elf_fill` allows the application to change that value.
- The application can generate its own data buffers to occupy the gaps, filling the gaps with values appropriate for the section being created. A program might even use different fill values for different sections. For example, it could set text sections' bytes to no-operation instructions, while filling data section holes with zero. With this technique, the library finds no holes to fill, because the application eliminated them.

System Services

`elf_begin` and related routines provide a higher-level interface to ELF files, performing input and output on behalf of the application program. These routines assume that a program can hold entire files in memory, without explicitly using temporary files. When reading a file, the library routines bring the data into memory and perform subsequent operations on the memory copy. Programs that read or write large object files with this model must execute on a machine with a large process virtual address space. If the underlying operating system limits the number of open files, then a program can use `elf_cntl` to retrieve all necessary data from the file, allowing the program to close the file descriptor and reuse it.

When processing a file, the library decides when to read or write the file, depending on the program's requests. Normally, the library assumes that the file descriptor remains usable for the life of the ELF descriptor. If, however, a program must process many files simultaneously and the underlying operating system limits the number of open files, then the program can use `elf_cntl` to let it reuse file descriptors. After calling `elf_cntl` with appropriate arguments, the program can close the file descriptor without interfering with the library.

All data associated with an ELF descriptor remain allocated until `elf_end` terminates the descriptor's last activation. After the descriptors have been terminated, the storage is released; attempting to reference such data results in undefined behavior. Consequently, a program that deals with multiple input or output files must keep the ELF descriptors active until it finishes with them.

Although the `elf_begin` interfaces are convenient and efficient for many programs, they might be inappropriate for some. In those cases, an application may invoke the `elf_xlate` data translation routines directly. These routines perform no input or output, leaving that as the responsibility of the application. By assuming a large share of the job, an application controls its input and output model.

COFF Files

COFF is an object file format that preceded ELF on some computer architectures (Intel, for example). For those architectures, when a program calls `elf_begin` on a COFF file, the library translates COFF structures to their ELF equivalents, allowing programs to read, but not to write, a COFF file as if it were ELF (see `elf_update`). This conversion happens only to the memory image and not to the file itself. The `ELF_C_NULL` command to `elf_update` updates only the memory image; you can use the `ELF_C_WRITE` command to modify the file as well. Absolute executable files (`a.out` files) require special alignment, which cannot normally be preserved between COFF and ELF. Consequently, you cannot update an executable COFF file with the `ELF_C_WRITE` command, although `ELF_C_NULL` is allowed.

After `elf_begin` is invoked, file offsets and addresses in the ELF header, the program headers, and the section headers retain the original COFF values. A program may call `elf_update` to adjust these values (without writing the file); the library then presents a consistent ELF view of the file. Data obtained through `elf_getdata` are translated (the COFF symbol table is present as ELF, and so on). Data viewed through `elf_rawdata` undergo no conversion, allowing the program to view the bytes from the file itself.

Although the ELF library supports COFF, programmers are strongly encouraged to recompile their programs, obtaining ELF object files. If source code is not available, then use `cof2elf`(1) to convert COFF object files to ELF (see "Conversion Commands" in Chapter 5.)

ELF Library Function Names

Names associated with the ELF library take several forms. Table 4-1 summarizes them.

Table 4-1 *ELF Library Function Names*

Name	Meaning
`elf_`*name*	These class-independent names perform some service, *name*, for the program.
elf32_name	Service names with an embedded class, 32 here, indicate they are applicable only for the designated class of files.
`Elf_`*Type*	Data types can be class-independent as well, distinguished by *Type*.
`Elf32_`*Type*	Class-dependent data types have an embedded class name, 32 here.
`ELF_C_`*CMD*	Several functions take commands that control their actions. These values are members of the `ELF_CMD` enumeration; they range from zero through `ELF_C_NUM-1`.
`ELF_F_`*FLAG*	Several functions take flags that control library status and/or actions. Flags are bits that can be combined.
`ELF32_FSZ_`*TYPE*	These constants give the file sizes in bytes of the basic ELF types for the 32-bit class of files.

Table 4-1 *ELF Library Function Names (Continued)*

Name	Meaning
ELF_K_*KIND*	The function elf_kind identifies the *KIND* of file associated with an ELF descriptor. These values are members of the ELF_Kind enumeration. They range from zero through ELF_K_NUM-1.
ELF_T_*TYPE*	When a service function deals with multiple types, names of this form specify the desired *TYPE*. Thus, for example, ELF_T_EHDR is directly related to ELF32_Ehdr. These values are members of the Elf_Type enumeration; they range from zero through ELF_T_NUM-1.

❑ Program Control Functions

Before the first call to elf_begin, a program must call elf_version to coordinate versions. Then, elf_begin, elf_next, elf_rand, and elf_end work together to process ELF object files, either individually or as members of archives. After obtaining an ELF descriptor from elf_begin, the program can read an existing file, update an existing file, or create a new file. elf_begin can operate on all files (including files with zero bytes), provided that it can allocate memory for its internal structures and read any necessary information from the file. Therefore, programs reading object files may call elf_kind or elf_getehdr to determine the file type (only object files have an ELF header). elf_getident retrieves file class information. Finally, a program may call elf_update to update the ELF descriptor before calling elf_end to terminate use of an object file.

This section describes basic ELF library functions.

- elf_version — Coordinates ELF library and application version
- elf_begin — Makes a file descriptor
- elf_next — Provides access to the next archive member
- elf_rand — Provides random archive processing
- elf_cntl — Controls a file descriptor
- elf_update — Updates an ELF descriptor
- elf_end — Finishes the use of an object file

elf_version

```
cc [flag . . .] file . . . -lelf [library . . .]
#include <libelf.h>
unsigned elf_version(unsigned ver);
```

The program, the library, and an object file have independent notions of the "latest" ELF version. The working version should be the same for all operations on a particular ELF descriptor. Changing the version between operations on a descriptor probably will not yield the expected results. `elf_version` allows a program to determine the ELF library's internal version. It further allows the program to specify the memory types it uses by giving its own working version to the library. Every program that uses the ELF library must coordinate versions, as described below.

The header file `libelf.h` supplies the version to the program with the macro `EV_CURRENT`. If the library's internal version (the highest version known to the library) is lower than that known by the program itself, then the library may lack semantic knowledge assumed by the program. Accordingly, `elf_version` will not accept a working version unknown to the library.

Passing the working version (*ver*) to `EV_NONE` causes `elf_version` to return the library's internal version, without altering the working version. If *ver* is a version known to the library, then `elf_version` returns the previous (or initial) working version number. Otherwise, the working version remains unchanged, and `elf_version` returns `EV_NONE`.

Figure 4-2 is an excerpt from an application program illustrating how the program is protected from using an older library.

Figure 4-2
***`elf_version`* Example**

```
if (elf_version(EV_CURRENT) == EV_NONE)
{
     /* library out of date */
     /* recover from error */
}
```

See "ELF Versions" on page 73 for additional information.

elf_begin

```
cc [flag ...] file ... -lelf [library ...]
#include <libelf.h>
ELF *elf_begin(int fildes, Elf_Cmd cmd, Elf *ref);
```

elf_begin makes a file descriptor. After a program obtains the descriptor, it can read an existing file, update an existing file, or create a new file. elf_begin uses an open file descriptor (the argument, *fildes*) for reading and writing. The initial file offset [see lseek(2)] is unconstrained, and the resulting file offset is undefined.

The *cmd* argument takes the following values.

ELF_C_NULL
: When a program sets *cmd* to this value, elf_begin returns a null pointer without opening a new descriptor. *ref* is ignored for this command. (See elf_next on page 84 and the examples below for more information.)

ELF_C_READ
: A program sets *cmd* to this value in order to examine the contents of an existing file. Depending on the value of *ref*, this command examines archive members or entire files. Three cases can occur.

- ▲ If *ref* is a null pointer, then elf_begin allocates a new ELF descriptor and prepares to process the entire file. If the file being read is an archive, then elf_begin also prepares the resulting descriptor to examine the initial archive member on the next call to elf_begin, as if the program had used elf_next or elf_rand to move to the initial member.
- ▲ If *ref* is a non-null descriptor associated with an archive file, then elf_begin allows a program to obtain a separate ELF descriptor associated with an individual member. The program should have used elf_next or elf_rand to position *ref* appropriately (except for the

initial member, which elf_begin prepares—see the example). In this case, *fildes* should be the same file descriptor used for the parent archive.

- If *ref* is a non-null ELF descriptor that is not an archive, then elf_begin increments the number of activations for the descriptor and returns *ref*, without allocating a new descriptor and without changing the descriptor's read/write permissions. To terminate a descriptor for *ref*, the program must call elf_end once for each activation. (See elf_next and the examples below for more information.)

ELF_C_RDWR

This command duplicates the actions of ELF_C_READ and additionally allows the program to update the file image (see elf_update). That is, ELF_C_READ provides a read-only view of the file, while ELF_C_RDWR allows the program to read *and* write the file. ELF_C_RDWR is not valid for archive members. If *ref* is non-null, then it was created with the ELF_C_RDWR command.

ELF_C_WRITE

A program sets *cmd* to this value in order to ignore previous file contents, presumably to create a new file. *ref* is ignored for the command.

The following figures illustrate the use of elf_begin.

- Figure 4-3 illustrates a prototype for reading a file.
- Figure 4-4 illustrates random archive processing.
- Figure 4-5 illustrates how you might create a new ELF file. The example is simplified to show overall flow.
- Figure 4-6 illustrates how you might update an existing ELF file. Again, the example is simplified to show overall flow.

Figure 4-3
Prototype for Reading an Object File
If the file is a simple object file, then the program executes the loop one time, receiving a null descriptor in the second iteration. In this case, both `elf` and `arf` have the same value, the activation count is two, and the program calls `elf_end` to terminate the descriptor. If the file is an archive, then the loop processes each archive member in turn, ignoring those members that are not object files.

```
if (elf_version(EV_CURRENT) == EV_NONE
{
     /* library out of date */
     /* recover from error */
}
cmd = ELF_C_READ;
arf = elf_begin(fildes, cmd, (Elf *)0);
while ((elf = elf_begin(fildes, cmd, arf)) !=0)
{
     if ((ehdr = elf32_getehdr(elf)) != 0)
     {
            /* process the file . . . */
     }
     cmd = elf_next(elf);
     elf_end(elf);
}
elf_end(arf);
```

Figure 4-4
Random Archive Processing
After identifying the file as an archive, the program repeatedly processes archive members of interest. For clarity, the example omits error checking and ignores simple object files. Additionally, the fragment preserves the ELF descriptors for all archive members; that is, it does not call `elf_end` to terminate them.

```
elf_version (EV_CURRENT);
arf = elf_begin(fildes, ELF_C_READ, (Elf *)0);
if (elf_kind(arf) != ELF_K_AR)
{
     /* not an archive */
}
/* initial processing */
/* set offset = . . . for desired member header */
while (elf_rand(arf, offset) == offset)
{
     if ((elf = elf_begin(fildes, ELF_C_READ, arf)) ==
0)
            break;
     if ((ehdr = elf32_getehdr(elf)) != 0
     {
            /* process archive member . . . */
     }
     /* set offset = . . . for desired member
header*/
}
```

Figure 4-5
Creating a New ELF File

```
elf_version(EV_CURRENT);
fildes = open("path/name",O_RDWR|O_TRUNC|O_CREAT,0666);
if ((elf = elf_begin(fildes,ELF_C_WRITE, (Elf *)0)) == 0)
     return;
ehdr = elf32_newehdr(elf);
phdr = elf32_newphdr(elf, count);
scn = elf_newscn(elf);
shdr = elf32_getshdr(scn);
data = elf_newdata(scn);
elf_update(elf, ELF_C_WRITE);
elf_end(elf);
```

Figure 4-6
Updating an Existing ELF File
The call to `creat` *truncates the file, thus ensuring that the resulting file has the correct size. Without truncation, the updated file might be as large as the original, even if information were deleted. The library truncates the file, if it can, with* `ftruncate` *[see* `truncate`*(3C)]. However, some systems do not support* `ftruncate`*, and the call to* `creat` *protects against that possibility.*

```
elf_version (EV_CURRENT);
fildes = open("path/name", O_RDWR);
elf = elf_begin(fildes, ELF_C_RDWR, (Elf *)0);

/* add new or delete old information . . . */

close (creat("path/name", 0666));
elf_update(elf, ELF_C_WRITE);
elf_end(elf);
```

Notice that both file creation examples open the file with write *and* read permissions. On systems that support `mmap`, the library uses it to enhance performance, and `mmap` requires a readable file descriptor. Although the library can use a write-only file descriptor, the application will not obtain the performance advantages of `mmap`.

elf_next

```
cc [flag . . .] file . . . -lelf [library . . .]
#include <libelf.h>
Elf_Cmd elf_next(Elf *elf);
```

`elf_next` provides sequential access to the next archive member. That is, having an ELF descriptor, *elf*, associated with an archive member, `elf_next` prepares the containing archive to access the following member when the program calls `elf_begin`.

After successfully positioning an archive for the next member, `elf_next` returns the value `ELF_C_READ`. If the open file was not an archive, if *elf* was null, or if an error occurred, then the return value is `ELF_C_NULL`. In either case, the return value may be passed as an argument to `elf_begin`, specifying the appropriate action.

elf_rand

```
cc [flag . . .] file . . . -lelf [library . . .]
#include <libelf.h>
size_t elf_rand(Elf *elf, size_t offset);
```

`elf_rand` provides random archive processing, preparing the ELF descriptor, *elf*, to access an arbitrary archive member. *elf* must be a descriptor for the archive itself, not for a member within the archive.

`elf_rand` returns the byte offset from the beginning of the archive to the archive header of the desired member. (See `elf_getarsym` on page 95 for more information about archive member offsets.) `elf_rand` returns 0 if an error occurred, if *elf* was null, or if the file was not an archive (no archive member can have a zero offset).

A program can mix random and sequential archive processing.

An archive starts with a "magic string" that has SARMAG bytes; the initial archive member follows immediately. Figure 4-7 shows how an application could rewind an archive. The function returns `-1` for errors and `0` otherwise.

Figure 4-7
***elf_rand* Example**

```
#include <ar.h>
#include <libelf.h>

int
rewindelf(Elf *elf)
{
      if (elf_rand(elf, (size_t)SARMAG) == SARMAG)
              return 0;
      return -1;
}
```

elf_cntl

cc [*flag* . . .] *file* . . . -lelf [*library* . . .]
#include <libelf.h>
int elf_cntl(Elf **elf*, Elf_Cmd *cmd*);

`elf_cntl` instructs the library to modify its behavior with respect to an ELF descriptor, *elf*. Generally, `elf_cntl` commands apply to all activations of *elf*. (Remember that an ELF descriptor can have multiple activations, and multiple ELF descriptors may share a single file descriptor.) If the ELF descriptor is associated with an archive file, then descriptors for members within the archive will also be affected, as described below. Unless stated otherwise, operations on archive members do not affect the descriptor for the containing archive.

If a program wishes to use the raw operations after disabling the file descriptors with `ELF_C_FDDONE` or `ELF_C_FDREAD`, described below, then it must execute the raw operations explicitly beforehand. Otherwise, the raw file operations will fail. Calling `elf_rawfile` makes the entire image available, thus supporting subsequent `elf_rawdata` calls.

If `elf_cntl` succeeds, then it returns zero. If *elf* was null or if an error occurred, then the function returns `-1`.

The *cmd* argument takes the following values.

`ELF_C_FDDONE`
: This command tells the library not to use the file descriptor associated with *elf*. A program should use this command when it has requested all the information it cares to use and wishes to avoid the overhead of reading the rest of the file. The memory for all completed operations remains valid, but late file operations, such as the initial `elf_getdata` for a section, will fail if the data are not already in memory.

`ELF_C_FDREAD`
: This command is similar to `ELF_C_FDDONE`, except that it forces the library to read the rest of the file. A program should use this command when it must close the file descriptor but has not yet read everything it needs from the file. After `elf_cntl` completes the `ELF_C_FDREAD` command, future operations, such as `elf_getdata`, will use the memory version of the file without needing to use the file descriptor.

elf_update

```
cc [flag ...] file ... -lelf [library ...]
#include <libelf.h>
off_t elf_update(Elf *elf, Elf_Cmd cmd);
```

`elf_update` causes the library to examine the information associated with an ELF descriptor, *elf*, and to recalculate the structural data need to generate the file image. (For a discussion on how COFF files are updated, see page 76.)

If `elf_update` succeeds, it returns the total size of the file image (not the memory image) in bytes. Otherwise, an error occurred, and the function returns `-1`.

The ELF_C_WRITE command (see below) translates data as necessary, before writing them to the file. The translation is not always transparent to the application program. If a program has obtained pointers to data associated with a file (see, for example, elf_getehdr and elf_getdata), then the program should reestablish the pointers after calling elf_update.

When updating internal structures, elf_update sets some members itself. Members listed in Table 4-2 are the responsibility of the application, and they retain the values given by the program.

Table 4-2 **Members Controlled by an Application**

	Member	Notes
ELF Header	e_ident{EI_DATA]	Library controls other e_ident values
	e_type	
	e_machine	
	e_version	
	e_entry	
	e_phoff	Only when ELF_F_LAYOUT asserted
	e_shoff	Only when ELF_F_LAYOUT asserted
	e_flags	
	e_shstrndx	
Program Header	p_type	The application controls all program header entries
	p_offset	
	p_vaddr	
	p_paddr	
	p_filesz	
	p_memsz	
	p_flags	
	p_align	
Section Header	sh_name	
	sh_type	
	sh_flags	
	sh_addr	
	sh_offset	Only when ELF_F_LAYOUT asserted
	sh_size	Only when ELF_F_LAYOUT asserted
	sh_link	
	sh_info	
	sh_addralign	Only when ELF_F_LAYOUT asserted
	sh_entsize	

Table 4-2 Members Controlled by an Application (Continued)

	Member	Notes
Data Descriptor	d_buf d_type d_size d_off d_align d_version	Only when ELF_F_LAYOUT asserted

Note that the program is responsible for three important members in the ELF header.

- The e_version member controls the version of data structures written to the file. If the version is EV_NONE, then the library uses its own internal version.
- The e_ident [EI_DATA] entry controls the data encoding used in the file. As a special case, the value may be ELFDATANONE to request the native data encoding for the host machine. An error occurs in this case if the native encoding does not match a file encoding known by the library.
- The sh_entsize section header member gives the size in bytes of each entry in a table of fixed-size entries. Although the library sets it for sections with known types, it cannot reliably know the correct value for all sections. Consequently, the library relies on the program to provide values for unknown section types. If the entry size is unknown or not applicable, then the value should be set to zero.

When deciding how to build the output file, elf_update obeys the alignments of individual data buffers to create output sections. A section's most strictly aligned data buffer controls the section alignment. To ensure proper alignment of each buffer, the library also inserts padding between buffers as necessary.

The *cmd* argument takes the following values.

ELF_C_NULL

This value instructs elf_update to recalculate various values, updating only the ELF descriptor's memory structures. Any modified structures are flagged with the ELF_F_DIRTY bit. A program thus can update structural information and then reexamine it without changing the file associated with the ELF descriptor. Because this process does not change the file, the ELF descriptor may allow reading, writing, or both.

`ELF_C_WRITE`

This value duplicates the `ELF_C_NULL` actions; `elf_update` also writes any "dirty" information associated with the ELF descriptor to the file. That is, when a program has used `elf_getdata` or `elf_flag` to supply new (or to update existing) information for an ELF descriptor, those data are examined, coordinated, translated if necessary (see `elf_xlate`), and written to the file. When portions of the file are written, any `ELF_F_DIRTY` bits are reset, indicating that those items no longer need to be written to the file (see `elf_flag`). The sections' data are written in the order of their section header entries, and the section header table is written to the end of the file.

When the ELF descriptor was created with `elf_begin`, it must have allowed writing the file. That is, the `elf_begin` command must have been either `ELF_C_RDWR` or `ELF_C_WRITE`.

elf_end

```
cc [flag . . .] file . . . -lelf [library . . .]
#include <libelf.h>
int elf_end(Elf *elf);
```

A program uses `elf_end` to terminate an ELF descriptor, *elf*, and to deallocate data associated with the descriptor. Until the program terminates a descriptor, the data remain allocated. *elf* should be a value previously returned by `elf_begin`; to simplify error handling, a null pointer is allowed as an argument. To write data associated with the ELF descriptor to the file, the program must use `elf_update` before calling `elf_end`.

A descriptor can have more than one activation. Calling `elf_end` removes one activation and returns the remaining activation count. The library does not terminate the descriptor until the activation count reaches zero. Consequently, a zero return value indicates that the ELF descriptor is no longer valid.

❑ Functions for Object File Parameter Data

This section discusses ELF library functions that provide information about parameters of object files that interest a program.

- ▲ `elf_fsize` — Returns the size of an object file type
- ▲ `elf_getbase` — Returns the base offset for an object file
- ▲ `elf_getident` — Returns file identification data
- ▲ `elf_kind` — Returns information about the file type

elf_fsize

```
cc [flag ...] file ... -lelf [library ...]
#include <libelf.h>
size_t elf32_fsize(Elf_Type type, size_t count, unsigned ver);
```

`elf32_fsize` returns the size in bytes of the 32-bit file representation of specified, *count*, data objects with a given type. The library uses a specified version, *ver*, to calculate the size. If the value of the specified type or the version is unknown, then `elf32_fsize` returns zero. (See Table 4-6 on page 112 for a list of type values.)

Constant values are available for the sizes of fundamental types, as listed in the table below.

Table 4-3 ELF Type Sizes

Elf_Type	File Size	Memory Size
ELF_T_ADDR	ELF32_FSZ_ADDR	sizeof(Elf32_Addr)
ELF_T_BYTE	1	sizeof(unsigned char)
ELF_T_HALF	ELF32_FSZ_HALF	sizeof(Elf32_Half)
ELF_T_OFF	ELF32_FSZ_OFF	sizeof(Elf32_Off)
ELF_T_SWORD	ELF32_FSZ_SWORD	sizeof(Elf32_Sword)
ELF_T_WORD	ELF32_FSZ_WORD	sizeof(Elf32_Word)

elf_getbase

```
cc [flag . . .] file . . . -lelf [library . . .]
#include <libelf.h>
off_t elf_getbase(Elf *elf);
```

elf_getbase returns the file offset of the first byte of the file or archive member associated with the ELF descriptor, *elf*. If the offset is not known or obtainable, then elf_getbase returns -1. To simplify error handling, a null *elf* is allowed; the return value in this case is -1. The base offset of an archive member is the beginning of the member information, not the beginning of the archive member header.

elf_getident

```
cc [flag . . .] file . . . -lelf [library . . .]
#include <libelf.h>
char *elf_getident(Elf *elf, size_t *ptr);
```

ELF provides a framework for various classes of files, where basic objects can have 32 bits, 64 bits, and so forth. To accommodate these differences without forcing larger sizes on smaller machines, the initial bytes in an ELF file hold identification information common to all file classes. Every ELF header's e_ident has EI_NIDENT bytes, with the interpretation listed in Table 4-4.

Table 4-4 ELF Header EI_NIDENT Byte Interpretation

e_ident Index	Value	Purpose
EI_MAG0 EI_MAG1 EI_MAG2 EI_MAG3	ELFMAG0 ELFMAG1 ELFMAG2 ELFMAG3	File identification
EI_CLASS	ELFCLASSNONE ELFCLASS32 ELFCLASS64	File class

Table 4-4 ELF Header EI_NIDENT Byte Interpretation (Continued)

e_ident Index	Value	Purpose
EI_DATA	ELFDATANONE ELFDATA2LSB ELFDATA2MSB	Data encoding
EI_VERSION	EV_CURRENT	File version
7-15	0	Unused, set to zero

(See "ELF Identification" in Chapter 2 for a description of the bytes.)

Other kinds of files also may have identification data, although they would not conform to e_ident (see elf_kind on page 92).

elf_getident returns a pointer, *ptr*, to the file's initial bytes. If the library recognizes the file, then a conversion from the file image to the memory image may occur. In any case, the identification bytes are guaranteed not to have been modified, though the size of the unmodified area depends on the file type. If *ptr* is non-null, then the library stores the number of identification bytes in the location to which *ptr* points. If no data are present, if the ELF descriptor is null, or if an error occurs, then the return value is a null pointer, with zero optionally stored through *ptr*.

elf_kind

```
cc [flag . . .] file . . . -lelf [library . . .]
#include <libelf.h>
Elf_Kind elf_kind(Elf *elf)
```

A program calls elf_kind to determine the file type associated with an ELF descriptor, *elf*. *elf* should be a value previously returned by elf_begin. A null pointer is allowed, to simplify error handling, and causes elf_getehdr, elf32_getehdr, and elf32_ehdr to return ELF_K_NONE.

The function returns one of the following currently defined values.

`ELF_K_AR` The file is an archive [see `ar`(4)]. An ELF descriptor may also be associated with an archive member, not the archive itself; then, `elf_kind` identifies the member type.

`ELF_K_COFF`
The file is a COFF object file.

`ELF_K_ELF`
The file is an ELF file. The program can use `elf_getident` to determine the class. Other functions, such as `elf_getehdr`, retrieve other file information.

`ELF_K_NONE`
The kind of file is unknown to the library.

Other values are reserved, to be assigned as needed to new kinds of files.

❑ Header and Table Functions

This section describes functions that retrieve header information or provide table access.

- ▲ `elf_getarhdr` — Retrieves an archive member header
- ▲ `elf_getarsym` — Retrieves an archive symbol table
- ▲ `elf_getehdr` — Retrieves a class-dependent object file header
- ▲ `elf_getphdr` — Retrieves a class-dependent program header table
- ▲ `elf_getshdr` — Retrieves a class-dependent section header

elf_getarhdr

```
cc [flag . . .] file . . . -lelf [library . . .]
#include <libelf.h>
Elf_Arhdr *elf_getarhdr(Elf *elf);
```

`elf_getarhdr` returns a pointer to an archive member header, if one is available for the ELF descriptor, *elf*. If no archive member exists, if an error occurs, or if *elf* was null, then `elf_getarhdr` returns a null value.

The header includes the following members.

```
char            *ar_name;
time_t          ar_date;
long            ar_uid;
long            ar_gid
unsigned long   ar_mode;
off_t           ar_size;
char            *ar_rawname;
```

An archive member name, available through `ar_name`, is a null-terminated string with the `ar` format control characters removed. The `ar_rawname` member holds a null-terminated string that represents the original name bytes in the file, including the terminating slash and trailing blanks as specified in the archive format.

In addition to regular archive members, the archive format defines some special members. All special member names begin with a slash (/), distinguishing them from regular members, whose names may not contain a slash. These special members have the names (`ar_name`) defined below.

/ This member, if present, is the archive symbol table. It is the first archive member. A program may access the archive symbol table through `elf_getarsym`. The information in the symbol table is useful for random archive processing (see `elf_rand` on page 84).

// This member, if present, holds a string table for long archive member names. An archive member's header contains a 16-

byte area for the name, which may be exceeded in some file systems. The library automatically retrieves long member names from the string table, setting `ar_name` to the appropriate value.

Under some error conditions, a member's name might not be available. Although this unavailability causes the library to set `ar_name` to a null pointer, the `ar_rawname` member is set as usual.

elf_getarsym

```
    cc [flag ...] file ... -lelf [library ...]
#include &lt;libelf.h&gt;
Elf_Arsym *elf_getarsym(Elf *elf, size_t *ptr);
```

`elf_getarsym` returns a pointer, *ptr*, to the archive symbol table, if one is available for the ELF descriptor, *elf*. If the archive does not have a symbol table, if an error occurred, or if *elf* was null, then `elf_getarsym` returns a null value. If *ptr* is non-null, then the library stores the number of table entries in the location to which *ptr* points. This value is set to zero when the return value is null. The table's last entry, which is included in the count, has a null `as_name`, a zero value for `as_off`, and `~0UL` for `as_hash`.

The symbol table is an array of structures that includes the following members.

```
char            *as_name;
size_t          as_off
unsigned long   as_hash;
```

The members have the following semantics.

`as_name` A pointer to a null-terminated symbol name resides here.

`as_off` A byte offset from the beginning of the archive to the member's header. The archive member residing at the given offset defines the associated symbol. Values in `as_off` can be passed as arguments to elf_rand to access the desired archive member.

as_hash A hash value for the name, as computed by elf_hash.

elf_getehdr Functions

```
cc [flag ...] file ... -lelf [library ...]
#include <libelf.h>
Elf32_Ehdr *elf32_getehdr(Elf *elf);
Elf32_Ehdr *elf32_newehdr(Elf *elf);
```

elf32_ehdr and elf32_newehdr retrieve class-dependent object file headers. A program can use elf_getident to inspect the identification bytes from a file.

For a 32-bit class file, elf32_getehdr returns a pointer to an ELF header, if one is available for the ELF descriptor, *elf*.

If no header exists for the descriptor, then elf32_newehdr allocates a "clean" one, but it otherwise behaves the same as elf32_getehdr. elf32_newehdr automatically sets the ELF_F_DIRTY bit (see elf_flag).

If no header exists (for elf_getehdr), if one cannot be created (for elf_-newehdr), if a system error occurs, if the file is not a 32-bit class, or if *elf* is null, then both functions return a null pointer.

The header includes the following members.

```
unsigned char  e_ident [EI_NIDENT];
Elf32_Half     e_type;
Elf32_Half     e_machine;
Elf32_Word     e_version;
Elf32_Addr     e_entry;
Elf32_Off      e_phoff;
Elf32_Off      e_shoff;
Elf32_Word     e_flags;
Elf32_Half     e_ehsize;
```

```
Elf32_Half      e_phentsize;
ELF32_Half      e_phnum;
Elf32_Half      e_shentsize;
Elf32-Half      e_shnum;
Elf32_Half      e_shstrndx;
```

(See "ELF Header" on page 11 for a description of the members.)

`elf_getphdr` Functions

```
cc [flag . . .] file . . . -lelf [library . . .]
#include <libelf.h>
Elf32_Phdr *elf32_getphdr(Elf *elf);
Elf32_Phdr *elf32_newphdr(Elf *elf, size_t count);
```

`elf32_getphdr` and `elf32_newphdr` retrieve class-dependent program header tables.

For a 32-bit class file, `elf32_getphdr` returns a pointer to the program execution header table, if one is available for the ELF descriptor, *elf*.

`elf32_newphdr` allocates a new table with a specified number of entries (*count*), regardless of whether a table existed previously, and sets the `ELF_F_DIRTY` bit for the table (see `elf_flag`). Specifying a zero count deletes an existing table.

◆ ***Note:*** This behavior differs from that of `elf32_newehdr`, allowing a program to replace or delete the program header table, changing its size if necessary.

If no program header table exists, if the file is not a 32-bit class file, if an error occurs, or if *elf* is null, then both functions return a null pointer. Additionally, `elf32_newphdr` returns a null pointer if *count* is zero.

The table is an array of `Elf32_Phdr` structure, each of which includes the following members.

```
Elf32_Word      p_type;
Elf32_Off       p_offset;
Elf32_Addr      p_vaddr;
Elf32_Addr      p_paddr;
Elf32_Word      p_filesz;
Elf32_Word      p_memsz;
Elf32_Word      p_flags;
Elf32_Word      p_align;
```

(See "Program Header" on page 42 for a description of the members.)

The ELF header's `e_phnum` member tells how many entries the program header table has (see `elf_getehdr`). A program may inspect that value to determine the size of an existing table; `elf32_newphdr` automatically sets the member's value to *count*. If the program is building a new file, then it is responsible for creating the file's ELF header before creating the program header table.

elf_getshdr and *elf32_getshdr*

`cc` [*flag* . . .] *file* . . . `-lelf` [*library* . . .]

`#include <libelf.h>`

`Elf32_Shdr *elf32_getshdr(Elf_Scn` **scn*);

`elf_getshdr` and `elf32_getshdr` retrieve class-dependent section headers. For a 32-bit class file, `elf32_getshdr` returns a pointer to a section header for the section descriptor, *scn*. If the file is not a 32-bit class, if *scn* was null, or if an error occurred, then `elf32_getshdr` returns a null value.

The header includes the following members:

```
Elf32_Word      sh_name;
Elf32_Word      sh_type;
Elf32_Word      sh_flags;
Elf32_Addr      sh_addr;
Elf32_Off       sh_offset;
Elf32_Word      sh_size;
```

```
    Elf32_Word      sh_link;
    Elf32_Word      sh_info;
    Elf32_Word      sh_addralign;
    Elf32_Word      sh_entsize;
```

(See "Section Header" on page 19 for a description of the members.)

If the program is building a new file, then it is responsible for creating the file's ELF header before creating sections.

❑ Data Retrieval Functions

The section describes functions that allow a program to retrieve section data.

- ▲ `elf_getdata`, `elf_newdata`, and `elf_rawdata` — Access and manipulate data associated with a section description
- ▲ `elf_getscn` — Provides access to section information
- ▲ `elf_rawfile` — Retrieves uninterpreted file contents

elf_getdata, elf_newdata, and elf_rawdata

```
cc [flag ...] file ... -lelf [library ...]
#include <libelf.h>
Elf_Data *elf_getdata(Elf_Scn *scn, Elf_Data *data);
Elf_Data *elf_newdata(Elf_Scn *scn);
Elf_Data *elf_rawdata(Elf_Scn *scn, Elf_Data *data);
```

`elf_getdata`, `elf_newdata`, and `elf_rawdata` access and manipulate data associated with a section descriptor, *scn*. When reading an existing file, a section has a single data buffer associated with it. A program can build a new section in pieces, however, composing the new data from multiple data buffers. For this reason, "the" data for a section should be viewed as a list of buffers, each of which is available through a data descriptor.

elf_getdata allows a program to step through a section's data list. If the incoming data descriptor, *data*, is null, then the function returns the first buffer associated with the section. Otherwise, *data* should be a data descriptor associated with *scn*, and the function gives the program access to the next data element for the section. If *scn* is null or if an error occurs, then elf_getdata returns a null pointer.

elf_getdata translates the data from file representation into memory representation (see elf_xlate) and presents objects with memory data types to the program, based on the files's class. The working library version specifies what version of the memory structures the program wishes elf_getdata to present.

elf_newdata creates a new data descriptor for a section, appending it to any data elements already associated with the section. The new data descriptor appears empty, indicating that the element holds no data. For convenience, the descriptor's type (d_type, see below) is set to ELF_T_BYTE, and the version (d_version, below) is set to the working version. The program is responsible for setting or changing the descriptor members as needed. elf_newdata implicitly sets the ELF_F_DIRTY bit for the section's data (see elf_flag). If the section argument, *scn*, is null or if an error occurs, then elf_newdata returns a null pointer.

elf_rawdata differs from elf_getdata by returning only uninterpreted bytes, regardless of the section type. The function typically should be used only to retrieve a section image from a file being read, and then only when a program must avoid the automatic data translation described below. Moreover, a program may not close or disable (see elf_cntl) the file descriptor associated with *elf* before the initial raw operation, because elf_rawdata might read the data from the file to ensure that it does not interfere with elf_getdata. (See elf_rawfile for a related facility that applies to the entire file.) When elf_getdata provides the correct translation, its use is recommended over elf_rawdata. If the *scn* argument is null or if an error occurs, then elf_rawdata returns a null pointer.

Elf_Data Structure

The Elf_Data structure includes the following members, which are available for direct manipulation by the program.

```
void            *d_buf;
Elf_Type        d_type;
size_t          d_size;
off_t           d_off;
size_t          d_align;
unsigned        d_version;
```

The members have the following meaning.

`d_buf` Points to the data buffer. A data element with no data has a null pointer.

`d_type` Specifies the type of data to which `d_buf` points. The section type determines how to interpret the section contents, as summarized below in Table 4-5.

`d_size` Holds the total size, in bytes, of the memory occupied by the data. The value may differ from the size as represented in the file. If no data exist, then the size is zero. (See the discussion of `SHT_NOBITS` in "Section and Memory Types" on page 102).

`d_off` Provides the offset, within the section, at which the buffer resides. The offset is relative to the file's section, not to that of the memory object.

`d_align` Holds the buffer's required alignment, from the beginning of the section. That is, `d_off` is a multiple of the member value. For example, if this member value is four, then the beginning of the buffer will be four-byte aligned within the section. Moreover, the entire section will be aligned to the maximum of its constituents, thus ensuring appropriate alignment for a buffer within the section and within the file. (See "Data Alignment" on page 75 for more information.)

`d_version`
Holds the version number of the objects in the buffer. When the library originally read the data from the object file, it used the working version to control the translation to memory objects.

Section and Memory Types

elf_getdata interprets section data according to the section type (see elf_getshdr). The following table shows the section types and how the library represents them with memory data types for the 32-bit file class. Other classes would have similar tables. By implication, the memory data types control translation by elf_xlate.

Table 4-5 Section Type Representation in Memory

Section Type	Elf_Type	32-bit Type
SHT_DYNAMIC	ELF_T_DYN	Elf32_Dyn
SHT_DYNSYM	ELF_T_SYM	Elf32_Sym
SHT_HASH	ELF_T_WORD	Elf32_Word
SHT_NOBITS	ELF_T_BYTE	unsigned char
SHT_NOTE	ELF_T_BYTE	unsigned char
SHT_NULL	none	none
SHT_PROGBITS	ELF_T_BYTE	unsigned char
SHT_REL	ELF_T_REL	Elf32_Rel
SHT_RELA	ELF_T_RELA	Elf32_Rela
SHT_STRTAB	ELF_T_BYTE	unsigned char
SHT_SYMTAB	ELF_T_SYM	Elf32_Sym
other	ELF_T_BYTE	unsigned char

The program's working version controls what structures the library creates for the application. The library similarly interprets section types according to the versions. If a section type is part of a version newer than the application's working version, then the library does not translate the section data. Because the application cannot know the data format in this case, the library presents an untranslated buffer of type ELF_T_BYTE, just as it would for an unrecognized section type.

A section with a special type, SHT_NOBITS, occupies no space in an object file, even when the section header indicates a non-zero size. elf_getdata and elf_rawdata process such a section, setting the data structure to have a null buffer pointer and the type indicated above. Although no data are present, the d_size value is set to the size of the section header. When a program is creating a new section of type SHT_NOBITS, it should use elf_newdata to add data buffers to the section. The empty data buffers should have the d_size members set to the desired size and the d_buf members set to null.

Figure 4-8 illustrates a fragment that obtains the string table holding section names; for simplicity, error checking is ignored. (See `elf_strptr` for a variation of string table handling.)

```
ehdr = elf32_getehdr(elf);
scn = elf_getscn(elf, (size_t)ehdr->e_shstrndx);
shdr = elf32_getshdr(scn);
if (shdr->sh_type != SHT_STRTAB)
{
      /* not a string table */
}
data = 0;
if ((data = elf_getdata(scn, data)) == 0 || \
 data ->d_size == 0)
{
      /* error or no data */
}
```

Figure 4-8
Retrieving String Table with Section Names
The `e_shstrndx` member in an ELF header holds the section table index of the string table. The program obtains a section descriptor for that section, verifies that it is a string table, and then retrieves the data. When this fragment finishes, `dat->d_buf` points at the first byte of the string table, and `data->d_size` holds the string table size in bytes.

`elf_getscn`, `elf_ndxscn`, `elf_newscn`, and `elf_nextscn`

`cc` [*flag* . . .] *file* . . . `-lelf` [*library* . . .]
`#include <libelf.h>`
`Elf_Scn *elf_getscn(Elf` **elf*, `size_t` *index*);
`size_t elf_ndxscn(Elf_Scn` **scn*);
`Elf_Scn *elf_newscn(Elf` **elf*);
`Elf_Scn *elf_nextscn(Elf` **elf*, `Elf_Scn` **scn*);

`elf_getscn`, `elf_ndxscn`, `elf_newscn`, and `elf_nextscn` provide indexed and sequential access to the sections associated with the ELF descriptor, *elf*. If the program is building a new file, then it is responsible for creating the file's ELF header before creating sections (see `elf_getehdr`).

elf_getscn returns a section descriptor, given an index into the file's section header table. Note that the first "real" section has index 1. Although a program can get a section descriptor for the section whose index is 0 (SHN_UNDEF, the undefined section), the section has no data and the section header is empty, though present. If the specified section does not exist, then an error occurs; if *elf* is null, then elf_getscn returns a null pointer.

elf_newscn creates a section and appends it to the list for *elf*. Because the SHN_UNDEF section is required but is not interesting to applications, the library creates it automatically. Thus, the first call to elf_newscn for an ELF descriptor with no existing sections returns a descriptor for section 1. If an error occurs or if *elf* is null, then elf_newscn returns a null pointer.

After creating a new section descriptor, the program can use elf_getshdr to retrieve the newly created, "clean" section header. The new section descriptor will have no associated data (see elf_getdata). When creating a new section in this way, the library updates the e_shnum member of the ELF header and sets the ELF_F_DIRTY bit for the section (see elf_flag). If the program is building a new file, then it is responsible for creating the file's ELF header (see elf_getehdr) before creating new sections.

elf_nextscn uses an existing section descriptor, *scn*, to return a section descriptor for the next higher section. You can use a null *scn* to obtain a section descriptor for the section whose index is 1 (skipping the section whose index is SHN_UNDEF). If no further sections are present or if an error occurs, then elf_nextscn returns a null pointer.

elf_ndxscn returns the section table index of an existing section descriptor, *scn*. If *scn* is null or if an error occurs, then elf_ndxscn returns SHN_UNDEF.

Figure 4-9 presents an example of sequential access.

Figure 4-9
Sequential Access Example
Each pass through the loop processes the next section in the file; the loop terminates when all sections have been processed.

```
scn = 0
while ((scn = elf_nextscn(elf, scn)) != 0
{
      /* process section */
}
```

elf_rawfile

```
cc [flag . . .] file . . . -lelf [library . . .]
#include <libelf.h>
char *elf_rawfile(Elf *elf, size_t *ptr);
```

A program may not close or disable the file descriptor associated with the ELF descriptor, *elf*, before the initial call to `elf_rawfile`, because `elf_rawfile` might have to read the data from the file if it does not already have the original bytes in memory. Generally, this function is more efficient for unknown file types than for object files. The library implicitly translates object files in memory, while it leaves unknown files unmodified. Thus, asking for the uninterpreted image of an object file may create a duplicate copy in memory.

A program that uses `elf_rawfile` and that also interprets the same file as an object file potentially has two copies of the bytes in memory. If such a program requests the raw image first, before it asks for translated information (through such functions as `elf_getehdr` or `elf_getdata`), then the library freezes its original memory copy for the raw image. It then uses this frozen copy as the source for creating translated objects, without reading the file again. Consequently, the application should view the raw file image returned by `elf_rawfile` as a read-only buffer, unless it wants to alter its own view of data subsequently translated. In any case, the application may alter the translated objects without changing bytes visible in the raw image.

Multiple calls to `elf_rawfile` with the same ELF descriptor return the same value; the library does not create duplicate copies of the file.

`elf_rawfile` returns a pointer, *ptr*, to an uninterpreted byte image of a file. This function should be used only to retrieve a file being read. For example, a program might use `elf_rawfile` to retrieve the bytes for an archive member. If *ptr* is non-null, then the library also stores the file's size, in bytes, in the location to which *ptr* points. If no data are present, if *elf* is null, or if an error occurs, then the return value is a null pointer, with zero optionally stored through *ptr*.

`elf_rawdata` is a related function, providing access to sections within a file.

❑ Utility Functions

- ▲ This section describes ELF library functions that a program can call to perform specific operations.
- ▲ `elf_error` — Handles errors
- ▲ `elf_fill` — Sets a fill byte
- ▲ `elf_flag` — Manipulates flags
- ▲ `elf_hash` — Computes hash values
- ▲ `elf_strptr` — Converts a string section to a string pointer
- ▲ `elf_xlate` — Translates class-dependent data structures

elf_error Functions

```
cc [flag ...] file ... -lelf [library ...]
#include <libelf.h>

const char *elf_errmsg(int err);
int elf_errno(void);
```

If an ELF library function fails, then a program can call `elf_errno` to retrieve the library's internal error number. As a side effect, the function resets the internal error number to zero, which indicates no error.

`elf_errmsg` takes an error number, *err*, and returns a null-terminated error message (with no trailing new-line) that describes the problem. A zero *err* retrieves a message for the most recent error. If no error has occurred, then the return value is a null pointer (not a pointer to the null string). A `-1` value of *err* also retrieves the most recent error, except that it guarantees a non-null return value, even when no error has occurred. If no message is available for the given number, then `elf_errmsg` returns a pointer to an appropriate message. The function does not have the side effect of clearing the internal error message.

Figure 4-10 exemplifies the use of `elf_error` functions.

Figure 4-10
***elf_error* Example**
This code fragment clears the internal error number and checks it later for errors. Unless an error occurs after the first call to `elf_errno`*, the next call will return zero.*

```
(void)elf_errno();
while (more_to_do)
{
      /* processing . . . */
      if ((err= elf_errno()) != 0)
      {
              msg = elf_errmsg(err);
              /* print msg */
      }
}
```

elf_fill

```
cc [flag . . .] file . . . -lelf [library . . .]
#include <libelf.h>
void elf_fill(int fill);
```

Alignment constraints for ELF files sometimes require the presence of "holes." For example, if data for one section are required to begin on an 8-byte boundary but the preceding section is too short, then the library must fill the intervening bytes. These bytes are set to a *fill* character. The library uses zero bytes unless the application supplies a value. (See "Data Alignment" on page 75 for more information.)

An application can assume control of the object file organization by setting the `ELF_F_LAYOUT` bit (see `elf_flag`). When that bit is set, the library does not fill holes.

`elf_flag` Functions

```
cc [flag ...] file ... -lelf [library ...]
#include <libelf.h>
unsigned elf_flagdata(Elf_Data *data, Elf_Cmd cmd, unsigned flags);
unsigned elf_flagehdr(Elf *elf, Elf_Cmd cmd, unsigned flags);
unsigned elf_flagelf(Elf *elf, Elf_Cmd cmd, unsigned flags);
unsigned elf_flagphdr(Elf *elf, Elf_Cmd cmd, unsigned flags);
unsigned elf_flagscn(Elf_Scn *scn, Elf_Cmd cmd, unsigned flags);
unsigned elf_flagshdr(Elf_Scn *scn, Elf_Cmd cmd, unsigned flags)
```

`elf_flagdata`, `elf_flagehdr`, `elf_flagelf`, `elf_flagphdr`, `elf_flagscn`, and `elf_flagshdr` manipulate the flags associated with various structures of an ELF file. Given an ELF descriptor (*elf*), a data descriptor (*data*), or a section descriptor (*scn*), the functions can set or clear the associated status bits, returning the updated bits. To simplify error handling, a null descriptor is allowed; all functions return zero for this degenerate case.

The *cmd* argument takes the following values.

`ELF_C_CLR`
: The functions clear the bits that are asserted in *flags*. Only the non-zero bits in *flags* are cleared; zero bits do not change the status of the descriptor.

`ELF_C_SET`
: The functions set the bits that are asserted in *flags*. Only the non-zero bits in *flags* are set; zero bits do not change the status of the descriptor.

The bits defined in *flags* are as follows.

`ELF_F_DIRTY`
: When the program intends to write an ELF file, this flag asserts that the associated information needs to be written to the file. For example, a program that wished to update the ELF header of an existing file would call `elf_flagehdr` with this bit set in *flags* and *cmd* equal to `ELF_C_SET`. A later

call to `elf_update` would write the marked header to the file.

`ELF_F_LAYOUT`

Normally, the library decides how to arrange an output file. That is, it automatically decides where to place sections, how to align them in the file, and so forth. If this bit is set for an ELF descriptor, then the program assumes responsibility for determining all file positions. This bit is meaningful only for `elf_flagelf` and applies to the entire file associated with the descriptor.

Note that when a flag bit is set for an item, it affects all subitems as well. For example, if the program sets the `ELF_F_DIRTY` bit with `elf_flagelf`, then the entire logical file is dirty. Figure 4-11 shows how you might mark the ELF header to be written to the output file.

Figure 4-11 *Marking ELF Header for Writing to Output File*

```
ehdr = elf32_getehdr(elf);
/* dirty ehdr . . . */
elf_flagehdr(elf, ELF_C_SET, ELF_F_DIRTY);
```

elf_hash

`cc` [*flag* . . .] *file* . . . `-lelf` [*library* . . .]
`#include <libelf.h>`
`unsigned long elf_hash(const char` **name*);

`elf_hash` computes a hash value, given a null terminated string, *name*. The returned hash value, *h*, can be used as a bucket index, typically after computing *h* mod *x* to ensure appropriate bounds. *name* is treated as an unsigned `char*` to avoid sign extension differences. Using `char*` eliminates type conflicts with expressions such as `elf_hash("name")`.

Hash tables can be built on one machine and used on another because elf_hash uses unsigned arithmetic to avoid possible differences in signed arithmetic on various machines.

The symbol hash tables of ELF files are computed by means of elf_hash. (see elf_getdata and elf_xlate). The hash value returned is guaranteed not to be the bit pattern of all ones (~0UL).

elf_strptr

```
cc [flag ...] file ... -lelf [library ...]
#include <libelf.h>
char *elf_strptr(Elf *elf, size_t section, size_t offset);
```

elf_strptr converts a string section offset to a string pointer. The ELF descriptor, *elf*, identifies the file in which the string section resides; the argument, *section*, provides the section table index for the strings. A program can call elf_getdata to retrieve an entire string table section. For some applications, doing so would be both more efficient and more convenient than using elf_strptr.

If *elf* is null, if *section* is invalid or is not a section of type SHT_STRTAB, if the section data cannot be obtained, if the offset is invalid, or if an error occurs, then elf_strptrl returns a null pointer.

Figure 4-12 presents a prototype for retrieving section names.

```
if ((ehdr = elf32_getehdr(elf)) == 0)
{
      /* handle the error */
      return;
}
ndx = ehdr->e_shstrndx;
scn = 0;
while ((scn = elf_nextscn(elf, scn)) != 0)
{
      char     *name = 0;
      if ((shdr = elf32_getshdr(scn)) != 0)
       name = elf_strptr(elf, ndx, (size_t)shdr-
>sh_name);
      printf("'%s'\n", name? name: "(null)");
}
```

Figure 4-12
Retrieving Section Names
The file header specifies the section name string table in the `e_shstrndx` *member. The code loops through the sections, printing their names.*

`elf_xlate` Functions

cc [*flag*...] *file*... -lelf [*library*...]
#include <libelf.h>
Elf_Data *elf32_xlatetof(Elf_Data **dat*, const Elf_Data **src*,
    unsigned *encode*);
Elf_Data *elf32_xlatetom(Elf_Data **dat*, const Elf_Data **src*,
    unsigned *encode*);

`elf32_xlatetom` and `elf32_xlatetof` provide class-dependent data translations. `elf32_xlatetom` translates various data structures from their 32-bit class file representations to their memory representations; `elf32_xlatetof` provides the inverse. This conversion is particularly important for cross development environments.

src points to the source buffer that holds the original data, and *encode* provides the byte encoding in which the file objects are (to be) represented. *encode* must have one of the encoding values defined for the ELF header's `e_ident[EI_DATA]` entry (see `elf_getident`).

If the data can be translated, then the functions return a pointer, *dst*, to the destination buffer for the translated copy. If an error, such as incompatible types, destination buffer overflow, and so on, occurs, then the functions return null.

The translation routines use the `Elf_Data` descriptor (described by `elf_getdata`), as follows.

`d_buf` Both the source and destination must have valid buffer pointers.

`d_type` Specifies the type of data to which `d_buf` points and the type of data to be created in the destination. The program supplies a `d_type` value in the source; the library sets the destination's `d_type` to the same value. The values are summarized in Table 4-6.

Table 4-6 ***Elf_Type* Values**

Elf_Type	32-bit Memory Type
ELF_T_ADDR	Elf32_Addr
ELF_T_BYTE	unsigned char
ELF_T_DYN	Elf32_Dyn
ELF_T_EHDR	Elf32_Ehdr
ELF_T_HALF	Elf32_Half
ELF_T_OFF	Elf32_Off
ELF_T_PHDR	Elf32_Phdr
ELF_T_REL	Elf32_Rel
ELF_T_RELA	Elf32_Rela
ELF_T_SHDR	Elf32_Shdr
ELF_T_SWORD	Elf32_Sword
ELF_T_SYM	Elf32_Sym
ELF_T_WORD	Elf32_Word

Translating buffers of type `ELF_T_BYTE` does not change the byte order.

`d_size` Holds the total size, in bytes, of the memory occupied by the source data and the size allocated for the destination data. If the destination buffer is not large enough, then the routines do not change its original contents. The translation routines reset the destination's `d_size` member to the actual size required, after the translation occurs. The source and destination sizes may differ.

`d_version`
Holds version number of the objects (desired) in the buffer. The source and destination versions are independent.

Translation routines allow the source and destination buffers to coincide. That is, `dst->d_buf` may equal `src->d_buf`. Other cases where the source and destination buffers overlap give undefined behavior.

5

UNIX Tools for ELF Files

In addition to the functions provided by the ELF library, the UNIX operating system provides tools specifically for ELF files: to convert COFF object files and OMF libraries to ELF format and to read or manipulate ELF (object) files. This chapter describes those tools.

- ▲ Conversion commands
  - `cof2elf` — Translates COFF object files to ELF object files
  - `cvtomflib` — Converts OMF libraries to ELF
- ▲ File information commands
  - `dump` — Prints out selected parts of object files
  - `lorder` — Generates an ordered listing of object files
  - `nm` — Prints the symbol table of an object file
  - `size` — Reports the number of bytes in sections or loadable segments of an object file
  - `strings` — Finds printable strings in an object file or binary
- ▲ File manipulation commands
  - `dis` — Disassembles object files

- mcs — Manipulates the comment sections of an object file
- strip — Removes symbolic debugging information and symbol tables from an object file

❑ Conversion Commands

This section describes the UNIX operating system commands that enable ELF library functions to be applied to non-ELF object files or libraries.

- ▲ cof2elf — Translates COFF object files to ELF object files
- ▲ cvtomflib — Converts OMF libraries to ELF

The cof2elf *Command*

In cases when source code is not available, use cof2elf(1) to convert COFF object files to ELF. cof2elf translates only COFF relocatable files. It does not translate executable or static shared library files for two reasons:

- ▲ The operating system supports executable files and static shared libraries, making translation unnecessary.
- ▲ Executable files and static shared library files have specific address and alignment constraints determined by the file format; matching the constraints with a different object file format is problematic.

Some COFF debugging information is not translated, though this does not affect the semantics of a running program.

The cof2elf command has the form

cof2elf [-iqV] [-Q{yn}] [-s *directory*] *files*

Use the options as described in Table 5-1.

Table 5-1 *Options to* **`cof2elf`** *Command*

Option	Use to:
`-i`	Ignore partial translation conditions and modify the file anyway. Normally, the files are modified only when full translation occurs. Without the `-i` flag, unrecognized data, such as unknown relocation types, are treated as errors and prevent translation.
`-q`	Suppress (-q for quiet) the messages that `cof2elf` otherwise prints for each file it examines, telling whether the file was translated, ignored, and so forth.
`-V`	Instruct `cof2elf` to print a version message on standard error.
`-Q`*arg*	Add identification information about `cof2elf` to the output files; specify *arg* as `y`. This information can be useful for software administration. Specify *arg* as `n` (the default), to add no such information.
`-s`*directory*	Save a copy of the original files in the specified *directory*, which must exist. (`cof2elf` modifies the input files and does not save files it does not modify.)
files	Specify *files* to be converted. The translation of specific COFF object files to ELF occurs in place; that is, the original file contents are modified. If an input file is an archive, then each member is translated as necessary, and the archive is rebuilt with its members in the original order. `cof2elf` does not change input files that are not COFF.

The `cvtomflib` *Command*

You can convert libraries of OMF objects to libraries of ELF objects by means of the `cvtomflib`(1) command. Doing so provides XENIX-system compatibility with application packages that provide only OMF libraries, which could not otherwise be used in an ELF-based environment.

In translation, the original order of objects within the library is retained. Each library is converted in the directory in which it is located. The converted library overwrites the original, unless the `-o` option is specified. To be safe, copy the original library before conversion.

The `cvtomflib` command has the form

`cvtomflib` [`-v`] [`-o` *outfile*] *library* [*library. . .*]

Use the options to do the following.

- Produce verbose output for each converted object (`-v` option). Without this option, `cvtomflib` does its work silently.
- Specify (`-o` option) a new name, *outfile*, for the converted library without changing the original. The option is available only when a single library is being converted.

❑ File Information Commands

This section describes the UNIX operating system commands that provide information about object files.

- `dump` — Prints out selected parts of object files
- `lorder` — Generates an ordered listing of object files
- `rm` — Prints the symbol table of an object file
- `size` — Reports the number of bytes in sections or loadable segments of an object file
- `strings` — Finds printable strings in an object file or binary

The `dump` Command

The `dump` command dumps selected parts of each of its object file arguments. `dump` attempts to format the information it dumps in a meaningful way, printing certain information in character, hexadecimal, octal, or decimal representation, as appropriate.

The command accepts both object files and archives of object files. It processes each file argument according to one or more options. You must provide at least one option.

The `dump` command has the form

`dump` *options file* ...

Use the options as described in Table 5-2.

Table 5-2 *Options to* **dump** *Command*

Option	Use to:
`-a`	Dump the archive header of each member of an archive.
`-C`	Dump decoded C++ symbol table names.
`-c`	Dump the string table(s).
`-D`	Dump debugging information.
`-f`	Dump each file header.
`-g`	Dump the global symbols in the symbol table of an archive.
`-h`	Dump the section headers.
`-L`	Dump dynamic linking information and static shared library information, if available.
`-l`	Dump line number information.
`-o`	Dump each program execution header.
`-r`	Dump relocation information.
`-s`	Dump section contents in hexadecimal.
`-T` *index* or `-T` *index1, index2*	Dump only the indexed symbol table entry defined by index or a range of entries defined by *index1, index2*
`-t`	Dump symbol table entries.
`-u`	Control how much translation occurs from COFF values to ELF. When reading a COFF object file, `dump` translates the file to ELF internally; the translation does not affect the file contents. Normally (without `-u`), the COFF values are preserved as much as possible, showing the actual bytes in the file. If you specify `-u`, then `dump` updates the values and completes the internal translation, giving a consistent ELF view of the contents. Although the bytes displayed under this option might not match the file itself, they show how the file would look if it were converted to ELF.
`-V`	Print version information.

You can modify the capabilities of the options by specifying the following modifiers in conjunction with an option.

`-d` *number* or `-d` *number1, number2*

Dumps the section number indicated by number or the range of sections starting at *number1* and ending at *number2*. You can use this modifier with `-h`, `-s`, and `-r`.

When `-d` is used with `-h` or `-s`, the argument is treated as the number of a section or range of sections.

When `-d` is used with `-r`, the argument is treated as the number of the section or range of sections to which the relocation applies.

For example, to print out all relocation entries associated with the `.text` section, specify the number of the section as the argument to -d. If `.text` is section number 2 in the file, then the command

```
dump -r -d 2
```

prints all associated entries.

To print out a specific relocation section, use

```
dump -s -n name
```

for raw data output or

```
dump -sv -n name
```

for interpreted output.

`-n` *name* Dumps information pertaining only to the named entity. You can use this modifier with `-h`, `-s`, `-r`, and `-t`.

When `-n` is used with `-h` or `-s`, the argument is treated as the name of a section.

When `-n` is used with `-t` or `-r`, the argument is treated as the name of symbol.

For example,

```
dump -t -n .text
```

dumps the symbol table entry associated with the symbol whose name is `.text`, where

```
dump -h -n .text
```

dumps the section header information for the `.text` section.

-p Suppresses printing of the headings.

-v Dumps information in symbolic representation rather than numeric. You can use this modifier with `-a` (date, user id, group id), `-f` (class, data, type, machine, version, flags), `-h` (type, flags), `-o` (type, flags), `-r` (name, type), `-s` (interpret section contents wherever possible), `-t` (type, bind), and `-L` (value).

When `-v` is used with `-s`, all sections that can be interpreted, such as the string table or symbol table, are interpreted.

For example,

`dump -sv -n .symtab` *file*

produces the same formatted output as `dump -tv` *file*, but

`dump -s -n .symtab` *file*

prints raw data in hexadecimal. Without additional modifiers, `dump -sv` *file* dumps all sections in file, interpreting all those that it can and dumping the rest (such as `.text` or `.data`) as raw data.

The `lorder` Command

The `lorder` command finds the ordering relation for an object library. `lorder` accepts as input any object or archive file, regardless of its suffix, provided more than one input file is specified. If there is but a single input file, then its suffix must be `.o`.

The standard output of `lorder` is a list of pairs of object file or archive member names; the first file of the pair refers to external identifiers defined in the second. You can process the output by means of `tsort`(1) to find an ordering of a library suitable for one-pass access by the link editor, `ld`.

Note that the link editor can make multiple passes over an archive in the portable archive format [see `ar`(4)] and does not require that `lorder` be used when an archive is built. However, using `lorder` can allow for more efficient access of the archive during the link edit process.

The following files are associated with `lorder`:

- *TMPDIR*/`*symref` — temporary files
- *TMPDIR*/`*symdef` — temporary files
- *TMPDIR* — usually `/var/tmp`, but can be redefined by setting the environment variable `TMPDIR` [see `tempnam` in `tmpnam`(3S)].

The lorder command has the form

`lorder` *file* `...`

where *file* is one or more object or library archive files specified as input.

The following example builds a new library from existing `.o` files.

```
ar -cr library 'lorder *.o | tsort'
```

The nm *Command*

The nm command displays the symbol table of each ELF or COFF object file specified on the command line. The file can be a relocatable or absolute ELF or COFF object file, or it can be an archive of relocatable or absolute ELF or COFF object files.

For each symbol, `nm` prints the information listed in Table 5-3. The command options control the output of `nm` (see Table 5-4).

Table 5-3 *Symbol Parameters Printed by* `nm`

Parameter	Meaning
`Index`	The index (in brackets) of the symbol.
`Value`	The value of the symbol is one of the following: a section offset for defined symbols in a relocatable file; alignment constraints for symbols whose section index is `SHN_COMMON`; a virtual address in executable and dynamic library files.
`Size`	The size in bytes of the associated object.
`Type`	A symbol's type: `NOTYPE` (no type was specified); `OBJECT` (a data object such as an array or variable); `FUNC` (a function or other executable code); `SECTION` (a section symbol); or `FILE` (name of the source file).
`Bind`	A symbol's binding attributes. `LOCAL` symbols have a scope limited to the object file containing their definition; `GLOBAL` symbols are visible to all object files being combined; `WEAK` symbols are essentially global symbols with a lower precedence than `GLOBAL`.
`Other`	A field reserved for future use, currently containing zero.
`Shndx`	Except for three special values, the parameter is the section header table index in relation to which the symbol is defined. These special values exist: `ABS` indicates that the symbol value will not change through relocation; `COMMON` indicates an unallocated block and the value provides alignment constraints; `UNDEF` indicates an undefined symbol
`Name`	The name of the symbol.

The `nm` command has the form

`nm [-oxhvnefurplVT]` *files*

Use the options as described in Table 5-4. Note that you can use the options in any order, either singly or in combination; they can appear anywhere in the command line. If you specify conflicting options, then the first is taken, the second is ignored, and a warning message is posted.

Table 5-4 *Options to `nm` Command*

Option	Use to:
`-o`	Print the value and size of a symbol in octal instead of in decimal.
`-x`	Print the value and size of a symbol in hexadecimal instead of in decimal.
`-h`	Cancel display of the output heading data.
`-v`	Sort external symbols by value before they are printed.
`-n`	Sort external symbols by name before they are printed.
`-e`	(Obsolete because of changes to the object file format; will be deleted in a future release.) Print only external and static symbols. The symbol table now contains only static and external symbols. Automatic symbols no longer appear in the symbol table. They do appear in the debugging information produced by `cc -g`, which can be examined by means of `dump`.
`-f`	(Obsolete because of changes to the object file format; will be deleted.) Produce full output. Redundant symbols (such as `.text`, `.data`, and so on) which existed previously do not exist; producing full output will be identical to the default output.
`-u`	Print undefined symbols only.
`-r`	Prepend the name of the object file or archive to each output line.
`-p[-l]`	Produce terse output that can be parsed easily. Each symbol name is preceded by its value (blanks if undefined) and one of the following letters: `U` (undefined); `N` (symbol has no type); `D` (data object symbol), `T` (text symbol); `S` (section symbol); or `F` (file symbol). If the symbol binding attribute is `LOCAL`, then the key letter is lower case. If the symbol binding attribute is `WEAK`, then the key letter is upper case (if you specify the `-l` modifier, then the upper case key letter is followed by an `*`). If the symbol binding attribute is `GLOBAL`, then the key letter is upper case.
`-C`	Print C++ names decoded.
`-V`	Print, on standard error, the version number of the `nm` command being executed.
`-T`	(Obsolete because of changes to the object file format; will be deleted.) Truncate the symbol name. By default, `nm` prints the entire name of the symbols listed. Because symbol names have been moved to the last column, the problem of overflow is removed.

The `size` Command

The `size` command produces segment or section size information in bytes for each loaded section in ELF or COFF object files. `size` prints out the size of the text, data, and `bss` (uninitialized data) segments (or sections) and their total. Because the size of `bss` sections is not known until link-edit time, `size` does not give the true total size of pre-linked objects.

`size` processes ELF and COFF object files entered on the command line. If an archive file is input to the size command, then the information for each object file in the archive is displayed.

When calculating segment information, the `size` command prints out the total file size of the non-writable segments, the total file size of the writable segments, and the total memory size of the writable segments minus the total file size of the writable segments.

If it cannot calculate segment information, then `size` calculates section information. When doing so, it prints out the total size of sections that are allocatable, non-writable, and not `NOBITS`, the total size of the sections that are allocatable, writable, and not `NOBITS`, and the total size of the writable sections of type `NOBITS`. (`NOBITS` sections do not actually take up space in the file.)

If `size` cannot calculate either segment or section information, it prints an error message and stops processing the file.

The `size` command has the form

`size [-F -f -n -o -V -x]` *files*

Use the options as described in Table 5-5.

Table 5-5 *Options to the* **`size`** *Command*

Option	Use to:
`-F`	Print the size of each loadable segment, the permission flags of the segment, then the total of the loadable segment sizes. If no segment data exist, then `size` prints an error message and stops processing the file.

Table 5-5 *Options to the* **`size`** *Command (Continued)*

Option	Use to:
`-f`	Print the size of each allocatable section, the name of the section, and the total of the section sizes. If no section data exist, then `size` prints an error message and stops processing the file.
`-n`	Print non-loadable segment or non-allocatable section sizes. If segment data exist, then `size` prints the memory size of each loadable segment or file size of each non-loadable segment, the permission flags, and the total size of the segments. If no segment data exist, then `size` prints, for each allocatable and non-allocatable section, the memory size, section name, and total size of the sections. If no segment or section data exist, then `size` prints an error message and stops processing.
`-o`	Print numbers in octal instead of in decimal.
`-V`	Print, on standard error, the version information for the `size` command.
`-x`	Print numbers in hexadecimal instead of in decimal.

The examples shown below are typical `size` output.

```
size file         2724 + 88 + 0 = 2812
size -f file      26(.text) + 5(.init) + 5(.fini) = 36
size -F file      2724(r-x) + 88 (rwx) + 0(rwx) = 2812
```

The `strings` *Command*

The `strings` command looks for ASCII strings in an object or binary file. A string is any sequence of four or more printing characters ending with a new-line or a null character. The command is useful for identifying random object files, among other things.

The `strings` command has the form

```
strings [-a] [-o] [-n number | -number] filename ...
```

and you can use its options to do the following:

- Look everywhere in the file for strings. If this flag (`-a`) is omitted, then `strings` looks only in the initialized data space of object files.
- Precede each string by its offset in the file (`-o` option).
- Specify *number* as the minimum string length rather than 4.

For backward compatibility, use -*number* in place of `-n` *number*. Similarly, the `-a` and a `-` option are interchangeable. The `-` and the -*number* variations are obsolete.

❑ File Manipulation Commands

This section describes the UNIX operating system commands that change or manipulate object files.

- `dis` — Disassembles object files
- `mcs` — Manipulates the comment sections of an object file
- `strip` — Removes symbolic debugging information and symbol tables from an object file

The `dis` Command

The `dis` command produces an assembly language listing of a specified file, which may be an object file or an archive of object files. The listing includes assembly statements and an octal or hexadecimal representation of the binary that produced those statements. Self-explanatory diagnostics indicate errors in the command line or problems encountered with the specified files.

On output, a number enclosed in brackets at the beginning of a line, such as `[5]`, indicates that the breakpoint-able line number starts with the following instruction. The line numbers are printed only if the file was compiled with additional debugging information; for example, the `-g` option of cc. (Currently, symbolic disassembly does not take advantage of additional information available if the file is compiled with the `-g` option.) An expression such as `<40>` in the operand field or in the symbolic disassembly, following a relative displacement for control transfer instructions, is the computed address within the section to which control will be transferred. A function name appears in the first column, followed by `()` if the object file contains a symbol table.

The `dis` command has the form

`dis [-o] [-V] [-L] [-s] [-d` *sec*`] [-D` *sec*`] [F`*function*`] [-t` *sec*`] [-1` *string*`]` *file . . .*

Use the options as described in Table 5-6. Note that the options are interpreted by the disassembler, and you can specify them in any order. If you specify the `-d`, `-D`, or `-t` options, then only those named sections from each file name you supply are disassembled. Otherwise, all sections containing text are disassembled.

Table 5-6 *Options to* `dis` *Command*

Option	Use to:
`-d` *sec*	Disassemble the named section as data, printing the offset of the data from the beginning of the section.
`-D` *sec*	Disassemble the named section as data, printing the actual address of the data. (Note: `-D` replaces the `-da` option.)
`-F` *function*	Disassemble only the named function in each object file specified on the command line. The `-F` option can be specified multiple times on the command line.
`-L`	Look up source labels for subsequent printing. The option is valid only if the file was compiled with additional debugging information; for example, the `-g` option of `cc`.
`-1` *string*	Disassemble the archive file specified by string. For example, you can issue the command `dis -1 x -1 z` to disassemble `libx.a` and `libz.a`, which are assumed to be in LIBDIR (usually `/usr/ccs/lib`).
`-o`	Print numbers in octal. The default is hexadecimal.
`-a`	Specify symbolic disassembly where possible. Symbolic disassembly output appears on the line following the instruction; symbol names are printed in C syntax.
`-t` *sec*	Disassemble the named section as text.
`-V`	Print, on standard error, the version number of the disassembler being executed.

The mcs Command

Use the mcs command to manipulate a section, by default the .comment section, in an ELF object file. You can add to, delete, print, and compress the contents of a section in an ELF object file, but you cannot add to, delete, or compress the contents of a section that is contained within a segment. mcs prints only the contents of a section in a COFF object file. If the input file is an archive, then the archive is treated as a set of individual files. For example, if the -a (append) option is specified, then the string is appended to the comment section of each ELF object file in the archive; if the archive member is not an ELF object file, then it is left unchanged.

If mcs is executed on an archive file, then the archive symbol table is removed, unless only the -p (print) option has been specified. You must restore the archive symbol table by executing the ar command with the -s option before the archive can be linked by the ld command. mcs produces appropriate warning messages when this situation arises.

Files associated with mcs are:

- *TMPDIR*/mcs* — temporary files
- *TMPDIR* — usually /var/tmp, but can be redefined by setting the environment variable TMPDIR [see tempnam in tmpnam(3S)].

The mcs command has the form

```
mcs [-a string[ [-c] [-d] [-n name] [-p] [-V] file ...
```

Use the options as described in Table 5-7. You must give mcs one or more options; it applies each of the options in order to each file.

Table 5-7 *Options to mcs Command*

Option	Use to:
-a *string*	Append *string* to the comment section of the ELF object files. If *string* contains embedded blanks, enclose it in quotation marks. Characters from supplementary code can be used in object files. You can specify comments using characters from supplementary code sets with the -a option

Table 5-7 *Options to `mcs` Command (Continued)*

Option	Use to:
`-c`	Compress the contents of the comment section of the ELF object files. All duplicate entries are removed. The order of the remaining entries is not disturbed.
`-d`	Delete the contents of the comment section from the ELF object files. The section header for the comment section is also removed.
`-n` *name*	Specify the name of the comment section to access if other than `.comment`. By default, `mcs` deals with the section named `.comment`. Use this option to specify another section. The section name specified in *name* must contain only ASCII characters.
`-p`	Print the contents of the comment section on the standard output. Each section printed is tagged by the name of the file from which it was extracted; for archive files, the format is filename`[`*member_name*`]` : and for other files *filename*: is the format.
`-V`	Print, on standard error, the version number of `mcs`.

Examples of the use of `mcs` are shown below.

```
mcs -p file           #Print file's comment section

mcs -a string file    #Append string to file's comment section
```

The `strip` Command

The `strip` command strips the symbol table, debugging information, and line number information from ELF object files; COFF object files cannot be stripped. Once the stripping process has been done, no symbolic debugging access is available for that file. Therefore, you would normally run `strip` only on production modules that have been debugged and tested. Then, you could use `strip` to reduce the file storage overhead taken by an object file.

If `strip` is executed on a common archive file, then, in addition to processing the members, `strip` removes the archive symbol table. Before the archive can be linked by the `ld` command, you must restore the archive symbol table by executing the `ar` command with the `-s` option. `strip` produces appropriate warning messages when this situation arises.

The symbol table section is not removed if it is contained within a segment, or if the file is either a relocatable or dynamic shared object. The line number and debugging sections are not removed if they are contained within a segment, or if their associated relocation section is contained within a segment.

The following files are associated with `strip`.

- *TMPDIR*/`strp*` — temporary files
- *TMPDIR* — usually `/var/tmp`, but can be redefined by setting the environment variable `TMPDIR` [see `tempnam` in `tmpnam`(3S)].

The strip command has the form:

`strip [-blrVx]` *file* `...`

You can use the options to control the amount of information stripped from the ELF object file and to print the version number.

- Strip only line number information and do not strip the symbol table or debugging information (`-l` option).
- Strip only line number and debugging information and do not strip the symbol table (`-x` option).
- Print, on standard error, the version number of `strip` (`-V` option).

The `-b` and `-r` options are obsolete and will be removed in the next release. Their use results in the same effect as the default behavior.

6

Source-level Debugging with `sdb`

The symbolic debugger `sdb` is a source-level debugging program that allows you to interactively reference variables and the program statements in which they occur by their symbolic names and line numbers in C source code. You can also use `sdb` to debug C and assembly language programs at the machine level.

You typically use `sdb` in two instances: post-mortem debugging and live process debugging.

- ▲ Post-mortem debugging — When the UNIX system aborts an executing program, you might see the message

  ```
  Memory Fault - core dumped
  ```

  meaning that the program tried to reference an illegal area of memory; for example, a pointer pointed somewhere wild. Or you might see

  ```
  Bus Error - core dumped
  ```

  meaning that an error, typically caused by scanning a non-terminated string, occurred.

The words "core dumped" mean that the system has stored a core image file of the process at the time of failure. (See "core Image File" on page 134 for information about the file.) You can use `sdb` to examine the file, usually by printing a stack trace: the function that was executing when the process died, the function that called it, and so forth. That way you can check each function for variables with unexpected values.

- Live process debugging — Programs can also fail by running to completion with unexpected results.

  You can use `sdb` to examine and change the values of variables as each statement in your program executes or as sections of the program execute up to preset breakpoints. You can trace back variables from these breakpoints and, in general, stop and restart your program as you see fit.

In a program that has aborted, `sdb` lets you examine the core image file, then start a live process in the same session, so that you can see what your program was doing up to the point at which it failed.

❑ Before Using `sdb`

Before you start using sdb, you should know

- more about the core file you may need to debug
- how to use `sdb` more effectively by compiling your C program with the `-g` option

`core` *Image File*

When the UNIX system aborts an executing program, it creates in your current directory (access permissions allowing) a file called `core` that contains the current memory image of the process at the time of the failure. The core image file, called `core`, contains all process information pertinent to debugging: contents of hardware registers, process status, and process data. The format of a core file is object-file specific. The size of the core file created by a process is user-controllable [see `getrlimit`(2)].

For ELF executable programs, the core file generated is also an ELF file, containing ELF program and file headers. The `e_type` field in the file header has type `ET_CORE`. The program header contains an entry for every loadable and writable segment that was part of the process address space, including shared library segments. The contents of the segments themselves are also part of the core image.

The program header of an ELF core file also contains a `NOTE` segment. This segment can contain the following entries. Each has entry name `"CORE"` and presents the contents of a system structure.

`prstatus_t`
: The entry containing this structure has a `NOTE` type of 1. The structure contains things from the operating system's u-area of interest to a debugger, such as the general registers, signal dispositions, state, reason for stopping, process ID, and so forth. The structure is defined in `sys/procfs.h`.

`fpregset_t`
: This entry is present only if the process used the floating-point hardware. It has a `NOTE` type of 2 and contains the floating-point registers. The structure is defined in `sys/regset.h`.

`prpsinfo_t`
: The entry containing this structure has a `NOTE` type of 3. It contains information of interest to the `ps`(1) command, such as process status, CPU usage, `nice` value, controlling terminal, user ID, process ID, the name of the executable, and so forth. The structure is defined in `sys/procfs.h`.

COFF executable programs produce core files consisting of two parts: the first section is a copy of the system's per-user data for the process, including the general registers. The format of this section is defined in the header files `sys/user.h` and `sys/reg.h`. The remainder of a COFF core image represents the actual contents of the process data space.

See Appendix B for a list of signals that cause a core image to be constructed in the current working directory.

The C Compiler -g Option

To use sdb to full advantage, compile your program with the -g option:

```
$ cc -g -o prog prog.c
```

-g tells the compiler and link editor to store in your executable information about the names of variables and functions in your program and their line numbers in your source code. When you have finished debugging a program, you can remove the debugging information with the strip command. (strip removes other information as well, so you may want simply to recompile the program without -g.)

If you compile without -g, your object file still must have a minimal level of symbolic information for the link editor's use. Basic information is limited to the name and address of global and static functions and variables. It does not include the types of the symbols, but it does provide enough information to determine if a symbol is a data symbol (variable) or a text symbol (function). Compiling with -g does not change the basic information, but it adds type information, names and locations of local variables, and line number tables.

You can combine files compiled with and without -g. For example, none of the library functions — like malloc — are compiled with -g. What you are able to do or see at any time depends on which file the program is in when it stops. You will be able to tell immediately whether or not the file was compiled with -g from the event notification (the source line is displayed with -g — you will see the assembly instruction otherwise). debug prints the "No -g information" warning only if *none* of the files in the executable were compiled with -g.

Note that cc will not let you compile with both -g and -O. Optimization can move code around and move variables into and out of registers in ways that are hard for debug to track. If you have to debug optimized code, it is generally less confusing to debug at the assembly language level.

Because optimization occasionally confuses sdb, it is strongly recommended that you do not compile your program with both -g and -O. However, there may be times when an unoptimized program that appears to have executed correctly will fail after it has been optimized. For example, an optimized program with an uninitialized variable will probably fail even though its unoptimized version produced an apparently correct result earlier. In situations like this, it is usually better to recompile the program with both -g and -O.

Although you will have to make some adjustments for optimization — for example, you may not be able to set breakpoints in all the places you set them before — you will be able to debug the program at the source rather than the assembly language level.

❑ Command Line Syntax

Execute the program that you compiled in the example on page 136:

```
$ prog
Memory Fault - core dumped
```

To examine the executable program and its core image, use the following command:

```
$ sdb prog
```

`sdb` accepts three command line arguments. The first is the name of the executable file to be debugged, or whose core image is to be debugged; it defaults to `a.out` when not specified. The second is the name of the core file to be debugged, defaulting to `core`. The third is a list of colon-separated directories containing the source files of the executable; the default is the current directory. In the example, the second and third arguments defaulted to the correct values, so only the first was specified.

You can also use `sdb` to *grab* an executing process. This command stops the process temporarily so that you can examine it under `sdb` control. Suppose, for instance, you are running the program `myprog` in the background. You notice that a portion of it is executing more slowly than you think it should. You want to look at that portion with `sdb` without killing the process.

Enter the command

```
$ sdb /proc/12345
```

where `/proc` is the UNIX system directory that contains information about each process currently active on your system, and `12345` is the process ID of the program `myprog`. (You can use the `ps`(1) command to determine the process ID of any process currently active on your system.) The process stops at the first system call it executes or signal it receives after the `sdb` command is invoked. You then use `sdb` to examine the values of variables, set breakpoints, resume execution, stop at breakpoints, and so on. When you quit `sdb`, control returns to the program. The process continues execution where it left off.

Occasionally, the `core` file of another program may be in the directory of an executable you want to run under control of `sdb`. When you specify a hyphen as the second argument

```
$ sdb myprog -
```

you tell `sdb` to ignore the core image file.

Ordinarily, `sdb` stops a live process when the process receives a signal. When you specify a signal number with the `-s` option

```
$ sdb -s 14 myprog
```

you tell `sdb` not to stop the process for that signal. The signal is passed to the process. Use `-s` if your program will receive and handle numerous signals.

When you use the `-w` option

```
$ sdb -w myprog
```

`sdb` lets you edit the executable or `core` file to be debugged.

❑ Interactive Commands

Table 6-1 summarizes, in alphabetical order, the `sdb` commands exemplified in this section. (See also "Summary of sdb Options and Commands" on page 157 for additional information and for other `sdb` commands.)

Table 6-1 *sdb Commands*

Command	Meaning	Page
!	Set the value of a variable or a register	145
?	Display value of a variable, searching backward in a file.	147, 152
/	Display value of a variable, searching forward in a file.	141
a	Announce a line or a function and its arguments.	150

Table 6-1 *`sdb` Commands (Continued)*

Command	Meaning	Page
`b`	Set a breakpoint.	148
`B`	List all breakpoints.	150
`c`	Continue execution.	149
`C`	Same as `c`, except pass back to the program the signal that stopped the program.	149
`d`	Delete a breakpoint.	150
`D`	Delete all breakpoints.	150
`e`	Change the current source file	146
`g`	Continue execution at a given line.	150
`i`	Step through one or more machine-level instructions.	149
`I`	Same as `i`, except pass the signal that stopped the program back to the program.	149
`l, p, w, z`	Display lines in a file	146
`m`	Set a watchpoint.	151
`q`	Quit `sdb`.	152
`r`	Run the program.	148
`R`	Run the program with no arguments.	148
`s`	Step through one or more program statements.	148
`S`	Same as `s`, except step over function calls.	149
`t`	Trace function calls.	140
`x`	Print the current instruction and values of all registers.	145

Entering Commands

When you use `sdb` to examine an executable file, it prompts you with an asterisk (`*`), to indicate that it is waiting for a command.

When you use it to examine a core image file, such as the one in the previous section, its output will look something like this:

```
sub:30:        z[i] = 0;*
```

sdb reports that the program quit at line 30 in the function sub() and displays the source text of the offending line. It then prompts you to continue.

Line numbers are always counted relative to the beginning of the file and include comments and blank lines. sdb has a notion of current file and current function and, when the file was compiled with -g, of current line. If you are debugging an executable file, sdb sets the current function and line to main() and the first line of main(), respectively. If you are debugging a core image file, sdb sets the current line and function to the last line and function that were executed — in the example, 30 and sub(), respectively. In the latter case, if the function was not compiled with -g, sdb prints a warning to that effect and displays the function name and the address at which the error occurred.

Once you have received the * prompt, you can proceed as you like. You can examine the core image file, for instance, or set a breakpoint and start a live process. The next three subsections look at tasks common to debugging core files and live processes: printing a stack trace, examining the values of variables, and displaying source files. Those tasks are generally the only things you can do in debugging core; a fourth subsection describes how you debug a live process.

Printing a Stack Trace

To trace function calls in a stopped process or a core image file, use the t command. The following example debugs a core file:

Figure 6-1 *Example of Tracing a Function*

```
*t
sub(x=2,y=3)         [prog.c:25]
inter(i=16012)       [prog.c:96]
main(argc=1,argv=0x7fffff54,envp=0x7fffff5c) [prog.c:15]
_start()
```

sdb's output shows that the function sub() at line 25 in the file prog.c was called with the integer arguments x and y from inter() at line 96. inter() was called from main() at line 15. main() is always called by a startup routine named _start(), and accepts three arguments, conventionally referred to as argc, argv, and envp.

argv and envp are pointers, so their values are printed in hexadecimal. Argument values are printed in hexadecimal regardless of type if the source file was not compiled with -g.

Examining Variables

You can display the value of a variable by entering its name followed by the / command:

```
*errflag/
```

Unless otherwise specified, variables are assumed to be either local to or accessible from the current function. To specify a different function, enter the name of the function and a colon before the name of the variable:

```
*inter:i/
```

sdb displays the value of the variable i in the function inter(). See "Displaying and Manipulating Source Files" on page 146 for more information on changing the current function.

To display the address of the variable i in inter(), you can specify

```
*inter:i=
```

An easier way to do it is to enter

```
*.=
```

The period tells sdb to look for the last variable entered. In this example it was i in inter(). The command

```
*./
```

tells sdb to redisplay the value of i in inter().

`sdb` supports a limited form of pattern matching for variable and function names.

The symbol `*` is used to match any sequence of characters of a variable name, the symbol `?` to match any single character. Consider the following commands:

```
*x*/
*inter:y?/
**/
```

The first command prints the values of all variables local to or accessible from the current function that begin with `x`. The second prints the values of all two-letter variables local to or accessible from the function `inter()` that begin with `y`. The last prints the values of all variables local to or accessible from the current function.

If you have multiple calls to a function, you can display the value of a variable in a given call by using a comma, as follows:

```
*inter:*,2/
```

That command displays the values of all variables in the second call to `inter()` from the top of the stack. The command

```
**:*/
```

displays the values of variables in each function on the call stack. Note that you cannot use the metacharacters `*` and `?` in any command that specifies a line number, or in the commands to call a function, change the current function, or set a watchpoint. Nor can you use them to match a file name.

`sdb` normally displays the value of a variable in a format determined by its type as declared in the source program. To request a different format, place a specifier after the `/`. The specifier consists of an optional length specifier followed by a format specifier.

The length specifiers are listed in Table 6-2.

Table 6-2 *`sdb` Length Values*

Length Value	Specification
`b`	One byte
`h`	Two bytes (half word)
`l`	Four bytes (long word)

The format specifiers are listed in Table 6-3.

Table 6-3 *`sdb` Format Values*

Format Value	Specification
`c`	Character
`d`	Decimal
`u`	Decimal unsigned
`o`	Octal
`x`	Hexadecimal
`f`	32-bit single-precision floating point
`g`	64-bit double-precision floating point
`s`	Assume variable is a string pointer and print characters starting at the address pointed to by the variable until a null is reached
`a`	Print characters starting at the variable's address until a null is reached
`p`	Pointer to function
`i`	Interpret as a machine-language instruction

To display the value of `i` in hexadecimal, enter

```
*inter:i/x
```

or, more simply,

```
*./x
```

provided `i` in `inter()` was the last variable entered.

The length specifiers are effective only with the format specifiers d, o, x, and u. If no length is specified, then sdb uses the length for the type of the object being examined. A number can be entered with the s or a format specifiers to control the number of characters printed. The s and a specifiers normally print characters until either a null is reached or 128 characters have been printed. The number specifies exactly how many characters should be printed. The command

```
*str/10s
```

tells sdb to print ten characters starting at the address pointed to by the variable str.

sdb also recognizes C structures, arrays, and pointers; therefore, the following commands are legal:

```
*array[2][3]/
*sym.id/
*psym->usage/
*xsym[20].p->usage/
```

The only restriction is that array subscripts must be a number, *, or a range. (A range is two numbers separated by a semicolon.) Note that as a special case

```
*psym[0]
```

displays the structure pointed to by psym.

You can display the contents of core locations by specifying their absolute addresses. The command

```
*1024/
```

displays the contents of location 1024 in decimal. As in C, numbers can also be specified in octal or hexadecimal so the above command is equivalent to both

```
*02000/
```

and

```
*0x400/
```

You can mix numbers and variables, so that

```
*1000.x/
```

refers to an element of a structure starting at address 1000, and

```
*1000->x/
```

refers to an element of a structure whose address is at 1000. For commands of the type `*1000.x/` and `*1000->x/`, `sdb` uses the structure template of the last structure referenced.

You can print the value of a specified register, say `r3`, with the command

```
*%r3/
```

The `x` command prints the current instruction and the values of all registers.

If you are debugging a live process, you can set the value of a variable or a register with the `!` command. For example, to set the value of the variable `i` to 10, enter

```
*inter:i!10
```

To set the value of the register `r3` to 10, enter

```
*%r3!10
```

The value can be a number, a character constant — specified by `'`*character* — or another variable. You can set a character to any of the C language escape sequences. The value must be well-defined. Expressions that produce more than one value are not allowed, except when assigning a structure to a variable of the same type. Numbers are treated as integers unless a decimal point or exponent is used, in which case they are treated as having the type `double`. Register values, except those for floating-point registers, are treated as integers. If the address of a variable is given, it is regarded as the address of a variable of type `int`. C language conventions govern any type conversions necessary to perform the indicated assignment.

Displaying and Manipulating Source Files

`sdb` makes it easy to debug a program without constant reference to a current source listing. You can use it to display, and perform context searches in, the source files of the executable you are debugging or whose core image you are debugging. The commands are similar to those of the UNIX system text editor `ed`. Like the editor, `sdb` recognizes the current file and current line. `sdb` also knows how the lines of a file are partitioned into functions, so it also recognizes the current function.

Five commands display lines in a file:

`l`	Prints the line corresponding to the current instruction.
`p`	Prints the current line.
`w`	Prints a window of ten lines around the current line.
`z`	Prints ten lines starting at the current line.
`control_d`	Prints the next ten lines.

When a line from a file is printed, it is preceded by its line number. You can use line numbers as input to some `sdb` commands.

`z` and `control-d` advance the current line by nine and ten, respectively. You can also use the `+` and `-` commands to move the current line forward or backward, respectively, a specified number of lines. If the last command displayed source, a carriage return advances the current line by one. Entering a line number by itself causes that line to become the current line. You can combine these commands with the display commands, so that

```
*15+z
```

advances the current line by 15, prints ten lines starting with the current line, then advances the current line by nine. Note that the current line determines the current function.

To change the current source file, use the `e` command. For example,

```
*e file.c
```

causes the named file to become current. The current line is set to the first line of the named file. If the first line of the file is a function, that function becomes current. Otherwise, there is no current function. If the directory of the file is not in the search path, use `e` to add its path name to the search path. The path name must be followed by a `/`:

```
*e /home/tm/
*e file.c
```

You can also change the current file with the command

`*e` *function*

which causes the named function to become the current function, and the file containing it to become the current file. The current line becomes the first line of the function. If the directory of the file containing the function is not in the search path, you must add its name to the search path as described above. Note that you can use this form of the `e` command to change the current function in a `core` file. Note, finally, that an `e` command with no arguments causes the names of the current function and file to be printed.

You can use two commands to search for instances of a regular expression in a file:

`*/`*regular expression*`/`
`*?`*regular expression*`?`

The first command searches forward through the file for a line containing a string that matches the regular expression; the second searches backward. In either case, the search wraps around. The current line becomes the line containing the matched string. The trailing `/` and `?` can be omitted, as long as they are not embedded in a command associated with a breakpoint. Regular expression matching is identical to that of `ed`.

Debugging a Live Process

You can use `sdb` to examine and change the values of variables as each statement in your program executes, or as sections of the program execute up to preset breakpoints. To do either of these things, you must set at least one breakpoint before you start the program — otherwise you will not be able to stop it. If, for example, you are stepping through your program on a statement-by-statement basis, you might set a breakpoint at the first executable line of `main()` by using the command:

```
*main:b
```

If the first executable line of `main()` is line 3 of your current file, the command

```
*3b
```

sets the breakpoint. The command

```
*b
```

sets the breakpoint if the line is the current line, and

```
*main:3b
```

sets the breakpoint if line 3 of the current file occurs in `main()`. You can set a breakpoint at any executable statement of a function compiled with `-g`, and at any function even if it was not compiled with `-g`. Of course, you can set as many breakpoints as you like before you execute the program, and as many as you like while the live process is stopped.

Now you are ready to run the program:

`*r` *args*

That command runs the program with the given arguments as if they had been entered on the shell command line. If no arguments are specified, then the arguments from `sdb`'s last execution of the program are used. You can start your program again in the same `sdb` session, creating a new live process, by specifying `r` without arguments. To run a program with no arguments, use the `R` command.

Once the program starts, execution continues until a breakpoint is encountered, a watchpoint condition occurs, a signal such as `INTERRUPT` or `QUIT` is received, or the process terminates. After an appropriate message is printed, control always returns to you.

Now that the program has stopped at the first executable line of `f4main`(), execute that line — step through it — with the `s` command:

```
*s
```

The S command acts in the same way except that it does not stop in called functions. Use it when you are sure that the called function works correctly and you want to test the calling routine. Both s and S take as an argument a count of the number of statements to be executed. At the first executable statement of main(), the command

```
*s 2
```

causes that and the next executable statement to be executed. Note that if you are single-stepping with s or S, and sdb reaches a function that was not compiled with -g, it will continue execution until a function is reached that was compiled with -g.

For these bugs, you can use the i command to run your program one machine-level instruction at a time. sdb ignores any signal that stopped the program. The I command does the same thing except that it passes the signal that stopped the program back to the program.

When you have finished stepping through the program, you can run it to another breakpoint. Once a live process has stopped, you can resume its execution with the c (for "continue") command:

```
*c
```

When you enter a line number before c

```
*9c
```

sdb places a breakpoint at the named line in your current file and resumes execution. When execution stops at that line, the breakpoint is deleted. In contrast, when you specify

```
*c 9
```

sdb continues execution until it encounters the ninth breakpoint . In either case, it ignores any signal that stopped the program.

The C command does the same thing, except that it passes the signal that stopped the program back to the program. That feature can be useful in testing user-written signal handlers. The -s option can be used on the sdb command line to specify the number of a signal that will automatically be sent to a live process without stopping it. You should also use it if your program will receive and handle numerous signals.

You can tell sdb to continue execution at a given line with the g command:

```
*3g
```

That command causes execution to resume at line 3 of the current file. `sdb` will resume execution at that line and skip two breakpoints with the command

```
*3g 2
```

You should be sure not to resume execution in a function different from that in which the process was stopped, or at a line that bypasses needed initializations. Generally speaking, avoid using `g` unless you are sure that the section of code you are skipping is bad.

Except for the breakpoint counts, the syntax of `c`, `C`, and `g` is identical to that of `b`.

```
*main:6c
```

tells `sdb` to continue execution until it reaches the breakpoint it set at line 6 in `main()`.

The syntax is also the same to delete breakpoints with the `d` command:

```
*main:d
```

tells `sdb` to delete the breakpoint at the first executable line of `main()`. If the `d` command is given by itself, breakpoints are deleted interactively; as the location of each breakpoint is printed, enter `y` or `d` to remove it. The `D` command deletes all breakpoints; the `B` command lists them.

`sdb` will set a breakpoint. When it reaches the breakpoint, it automatically performs a sequence of commands if the `b` command is specified with an *associated command*:

```
*12b t;x/;c
```

This command directs `sdb` to first set a breakpoint at line 12 of the current file, and then to print a stack trace and display the value of the variable `x` each time it reaches the breakpoint. Use the `a` (for "announce") command to do something similar:

```
*function:a
```

instructs `sdb` to print the name of the specified function and its arguments each time it is called. The command

```
*function:12a
```

tells sdb to print line 12 in the specified function each time the line is about to be executed.

You can call a function in either of two ways:

```
*proc(arg1, arg2, ...)
*proc(arg1, arg2, ...)/m
```

The first command simply executes the function, the second executes the function and displays the value it returns. The value is printed in decimal unless some other format is specified by *m*. Arguments to functions can be register names, integers, floating point, character, or string constants, or variables local to or accessible from the current function. You can use this feature to test the same function with different arguments or to call a user-supplied function that prints structured data.

Finally, you can use watchpoints to monitor changes in the value of a variable or the contents of an address. In the former case, you set the watchpoint with the command

```
*x$m
```

where x is the variable to be monitored; in the latter, with the command

```
*1024:m
```

where 1024 is the address to be monitored. sdb begins single-stepping, as with the s command, and stops when the value of the variable or the contents of the address have changed. If they have changed, or if the process stops for any other reason, including a breakpoint, then the watchpoint is deleted automatically. The variable must be local to or accessible from the current function.

Debugging Machine-Level Instructions

You can use the i or I commands to step through your program one machine-level instruction at a time. These and the commands described below effectively disassemble your program for machine-level debugging. You can use sdb to display the machine language statements associated with a line in your source program and to place breakpoints at arbitrary addresses. You can also use it to display or modify the contents of machine registers, as described in "Examining Variables" on page 141.

for example, to display the machine language statements associated with line 25 in `main()`, use the command

```
*main:25?
```

The `?` command is identical to the `/` command except that it displays from text space. The default format for printing text space is given by the `i` specifier, described in "Examining Variables." Use `control-d` to print the next ten instructions.

Absolute addresses can be specified instead of line numbers by appending a colon to them, so that

```
*0x1024:?
```

displays the instruction at address 0x1024 in text space. Note that the command

```
*0x1024?
```

displays the first instruction corresponding to line 0x1024 in the current file.

You can set or delete a breakpoint by specifying its absolute address:

```
*0x1024:b
```

for example, sets a breakpoint at address 0x1024.

As noted, the `x` command prints the current instruction and the values of all registers; `X` prints the current instruction.

Exiting

To quit `sdb`, use the `q` command:

```
*q
```

The `!` command, when used immediately after the `*` prompt, is identical to that in `ed` and is used to execute a shell command. Other commands are described in `sdb`(1).

❑ Example of Debugging with `sdb`

The source code for the example is shown in Figure 6-2. The program consists of a `main()` routine and a recursively called function `foo()`. The number of calls to `foo()` is determined by the argument passed in `argv[1]`. For example, an argument of `50` causes 50 calls to `foo()`, and an argument of `150` causes 150 calls. Line numbers have been inserted in the source code and comments are placed in the `sdb` output to help you follow the session. Note that the example is for the 3B2. Register names and other processor-specific information would be different on an Intel386™ microprocessor.

Figure 6-3 shows how you can use `sdb` to debug an aborted program.

Figure 6-2
Source Program ***c_recurse.c***

```
#define          DEFAULT_MAX      150
int call_max;
int ab_val = 0;

void foo(int);

main(argc, argv)
int argc;
char *argv[];
{
     int start_stack=1;

     if (argc  < 2)
                 call_max = DEFAULT_MAX;
     else
                 call_max = atoi(argv[1]);

     foo (start_stack);

}

void foo(keepcalling)
int keepcalling;
{

     if (keepcalling  <= call_max) {
                 if (keepcalling == 8)
                         /* forces a core dump, for example */
                         ab_val = keepcalling/ab_val;
                 else {
                         keepcalling++;
                         foo(keepcalling);
                 }
     }
     return;
}
```

Figure 6-3
sdb Usage Example

```
$ cc -g c_recurse.c
$ a.out
Arithmetic Exception - core dumped
$ sdb
29:                    ab_val = keepcalling/ab_val;
*t                            # print stack trace
foo(keepcalling=8)     [c_recurse.c:29]
foo(keepcalling=8)     [c_recurse.c:32]
foo(keepcalling=7)     [c_recurse.c:32]
foo(keepcalling=6)     [c_recurse.c:32]
foo(keepcalling=5)     [c_recurse.c:32]
foo(keepcalling=4)     [c_recurse.c:32]
foo(keepcalling=3)     [c_recurse.c:32]
foo(keepcalling=2)     [c_recurse.c:32]
main(argc=1,argv=0xc00201c0,0xc00201c8) [c_recurse.c:18]
_start()
*x                            # print register set and current instruction
%r0          0x1        %r1          0x180     %r2          0x25
%r3       0x7d3    %r4           0        %r5  0x8001ef8a
%r6     0x8001ef0f       %r7     0x8001ef8a      %r8    0x8001ed14
%fp     0xc00203c8       %ap     0xc00203a0      %psw       0x1f03
%sp     0xc00203c8       %pcbp   0xc000007c      %isp            0
%pc     0x8000044e       %asr    0x80000000
%dr     0x00020000_02000000_00000000 = 0
%x0     0x00000000_00000000_00000000 = 0
%x1     0x00000000_00000000_00000000 = 0
%x2     0x00000000_00000000_00000000 = 0
%x3     0x00000000_00000000_00000000 = 0
0x8000044e (foo:29)    DIVW3   $0x8000247c,(%ap),%r0  [0x8000247c,(%ap),%r0]
*l                            # print line corresponding to current instruction
29:                    ab_val = keepcalling/ab_val;
*X                            # print current instruction
0x8000044e (foo:29)    DIVW3   $0x8000247c,(%ap),%r0  [0x8000247c,(%ap),%r0]
*p                            # print current line
29:                    ab_val = keepcalling/ab_val;
*keepcalling/                 # print value of keepcalling, all foos
foo:keepcalling/8
foo:keepcalling/8
foo:keepcalling/7
foo:keepcalling/6
foo:keepcalling/5
foo:keepcalling/4
foo:keepcalling/3
```

```
foo:keepcalling/2
*foo:*,1                    # print values of all variables, top foo
foo:keepcalling/8
foo:ab_val/0
Assuming foo:main is int
foo:main/0x10499c4f
Assuming foo:foo is int
foo:foo/0x10499c4f
foo:call_max/150
:ab_val/0
Assuming :main is int
:main/0x10499c4f
Assuming :foo is int
:foo/0x10499c4f
:call_max/150
*foo:keepcalling,3          # print value of keepcalling, third foo
foo:keepcalling/7
*foo:ab_val,1/x             # print ab_val in hex format, top foo
foo:ab_val/0
:ab_val/0
*foo:b                      # set a breakpoint
0x80000437   c_recurse.c:24     foo
*r 10                       # run with an argument of 10 calls to foo
BREAKPOINT process 12465 function foo() in c_recurse.c
24:     {
*c 7                        # continue to 7th breakpoint
BREAKPOINT process 12465 function foo() in c_recurse.c
24:     {
*s                          # single step to see error
STEPPED process 12465 function foo() in c_recurse.c
26:             if (keepcalling  <= call_max) {
*foo:keepcalling,1          # check keepcalling -- is value 8?
foo:keepcalling/8
*w                          # see the code--confirm offending lines 27 & 29
21:
22:     void foo (keepcalling)
23:     int keepcalling;
24:     {
25:
26:             if (keepcalling  <= call_max) {
27:                 if (keepcalling == 8)
28:                     /* forces a core dump, for example */
29:                     ab_val = keepcalling/ab_val;
```

```
30:                    else {
*keepcalling!9                    # set to 9 instead of 8, avoid dump at line 29
foo:keepcalling/9
foo:keepcalling/8
foo:keepcalling/7
foo:keepcalling/6
foo:keepcalling/5
foo:keepcalling/4
foo:keepcalling/3
foo:keepcalling/2
*c;c;c                            # should terminate normally, could quit here
BREAKPOINT process 12465 function foo() in c_recurse.c
24:      {
BREAKPOINT process 12465 function foo() in c_recurse.c
24:      {
Process 12465 has terminated.
*q                                # know the problem, quit sdb
```

❑ Summary of sdb Options and Commands

This section summarizes sdb options and commands, some of which were discussed in the preceding sections. See also sdb(1) for more detailed information.

sdb *Options*

sdb [-e][-s *signo*][-V][-W][*objfile*[*corfile* [*directory-list*]]]

The sdb options have the following meaning.

-e Ignore symbolic information and treat nonsymbolic addresses as file offset.

`-s` *signo* Do not stop live processes that receive *signo* while under control of `sdb`, where *signo* is a decimal number that corresponds to a signal number (see Table B-1). You can use the option more than once on the `sdb` command line.

-V Print version information. If no *objfile* argument is specified on the command line, then `sdb` exits after printing the version information.

`-W` Suppress warnings about *corfile* being older than *objfile* or about source files that are older than *objfile*.

`-w` Allow user to write to *objfile* or *corfile*.

objfile The name of an executable program file. If *objfile* is a dynamically linked executable, then variables, function names, and so forth that are defined in shared objects cannot be referenced until the shared object in which the variables et al. are defined is attached to the process. For shared objects attached at startup, the implication is that such variables are not accessible until `main` is called.

corfile The name of a core image file, `core` by default.

directory-list
A colon-separated list of directories used to locate the source files that built *objfile*. If no directory list is specified, then `sdb` looks in the current directory.

`sdb` *Commands*

The following tables summarize the commands that can be entered at the `sdb` prompt, * (asterisk).

- Table 6-4 — Commands for examining data in a program
- Table 6-5 — Commands for examining source files
- Table 6-6 — Commands for controlling execution of a source program
- Table 6-7 — Miscellaneous commands

Table 6-4 *Commands for Examining Data in a Program*

Command	Use to:
`t`	Print a stack trace of the terminated or halted program. The function invoked most recently is at the top of the stack.
`T`	Print the top line of the stack trace.
variable/*clm*	Print the value of variable according to length *l* and format *m*, as described in Table 6-2 and Table 6-3. The numeric count *c* indicates that a region of memory, beginning at the address implied by *variable*, is to be displayed.
linenumber?*lm* *variable*:?*lm*	Print the value at the address from the executable or text space given by *linenumber* or *variable* (procedure name), according to the format *lm*. The default format is `i`.
variable=*lm* *linenumber*=*lm* *number*=*lm*	Print the address of *variable* or *linenumber* or the value of number according the format *lm*. If you do not specify a format, then `sdb` uses `lx`; that is, four-byte hex.
variable!*value*	Set variable to the specified value. The value can be a number, a character constant, or a variable., but must be well-defined.
`x`	Print the machine registers and the current machine-language instruction.
`X`	Print the current machine-language instruction.

Table 6-5 *Commands for Examining Source Files*

Command	Use to:
`e` `e` *procedure* `e` *filename* `e` *directory*/	Print the name of the current file. Set the current file to the file containing *procedure*. Set the current file to *filename*. Source files are assumed to be in the directories in the directory list. Add *directory* to the end of the directory list.
/*regular expression*/ ?*regular expression*?	Search forward or backward, respectively, from the current line for a line containing a string matching *regular expression*. You can omit the trailing / or ?, except when it is associated with a breakpoint.
`p`	Print the current line.
`z`	Print the current line and the following nine lines and set the current line to the last line printed.

Table 6-5 *Commands for Examining Source Files (Continued)*

Command	Use to:
`w`	Print the ten lines (the window) around the current line.
number	Specify the current line; print the new current line.
count+	Advance the current line by *count* lines; print the new current line.
count-	Reset the current line by *count* lines back; print the new current line.

Table 6-6 *Commands for Controlling Source Program Execution*

Command	Use to:
count `r` *args* *count* `R`	Run a program with the given arguments. If no arguments are specified, then reuse the previous arguments to the program. Run the program with no arguments.
linenumber `c` *count* *linenumber* `C` *count*	Continue execution. If *count* = 1, then the program stops at the next breakpoint. The signal that stopped the program is reactivated with the `C` command and ignored with the `c` command. If you specify a line number, then a temporary breakpoint is placed at the line, and execution continues; the breakpoint is deleted when the command finishes.
linenumber `g` *count*	Continue with execution resumed at the given line. *count* specifies the number of breakpoints to be ignored. If `count` = 1, then the program stops at the next breakpoint.
`s` *count* `S` *count*	Step the program through *count* lines. If you do not specify *count*, then the program runs for one line. The `s` command steps from one function into a called function. Step a program but do not step into a called function. Instead, step over the function called.
`i` *count* `I` *count*	Single step by *count* machine-language instructions. The `i` command ignores the signal that caused the program to stop; the `I` command reactivates the signal.

Table 6-6 *Commands for Controlling Source Program Execution (Continued)*

Command	Use to:
variable`$m` *count* *address*`:m` *count*	Single step until the specified location is modified. If you omit *count*, then the value is, in effect, infinity. *variable* must be accessible from the current procedure. Note: The command can be very slow.
level `v`	Toggle verbose mode. Use when single stepping with `S`, `s`, or `m`. If *level* is omitted, then just the current source file and/or function name is printed when either changes. If *level* is 1 or greater, then each C source line is printed before it executes. If *level* is 2 or greater, then each assembler statement is also printed.
k	Kill the program being debugged.
procedure(arg1, arg2, …) *procedure(arg1,arg2,…)/m;*	Execute the named procedure with the given arguments. Arguments can be register names, integer, character, or string constants, or names of variables accessible from the current procedure. Cause the value returned by the procedure to be printed according to format *m*; default format is `d`.
linenumber b *commands*	Set a breakpoint at the given line. If no *linenumber* is given, then a breakpoint is placed at the current line. If no *commands* are given, then execution stops at the breakpoint and control is returned to `sdb`. Separate multiple commands with a semicolon.
`B`	Print a list of the currently active breakpoints.
linenumber `d`	Delete a breakpoint at the given line. If you do not specify *linenumber*, then `sdb` deletes breakpoints interactively.
`D`	Delete all breakpoints.
`l`	Print the last executed line.
linenumber `a`	Announce a line number.

Table 6-7 *Miscellaneous Commands*

Command	Use to:
`#`*rest-of-line*	Instruct `sdb` to ignore comments.
`!`*command*	Instruct `sh` to interpret *command*.

Table 6-7 *Miscellaneous Commands (Continued)*

Command	Use to:
`new-line`	a) If the previous command printed a source line, then advance the current line by one line and print the new current line. b) If the previous command displayed a memory location, then display the next memory location. c) If the previous command disassembled an instruction, then disassemble the next instruction.
end-of-file character	Scroll the next ten lines of instructions, source, or data, depending on which was last printed. The end-of-file character is usually `control_d`.
<filename	Read commands from *filename* until the end of file is reach; then continue to accept commands from standard input. The command cannot be nested, and < cannot appear as a command in a file.
`M`	Print the address maps.
"string"	Print the given string. You can omit the trailing quote.
`q`	Exit the debugger.
`V`	Print version stamping information.

7

System Traces

System V Release 4 provides new facilities for inspecting and modifying the activity of running processes. These make it possible to implement sophisticated debuggers and other applications that control and report on details of process activity that were difficult or impossible to deal with through the older interface (the `ptrace`(2) system call).

This section describes:

- `/proc` — the new file system interface that provides access to running processes through standard I/O system calls
- `truss`(1) — a new application (implemented using the `/proc` facilities) that traces process execution and provides information about system calls, signals, and machine faults

❑ Active Process Traces through `/proc`

The file system `/proc` permits access to an image of each active process in the system.

/proc Overview

This section provides information that you should know when working with /proc files.

Access to /proc Files

The name of each entry in the /proc directory is a decimal number corresponding to the process ID. The owner of each "file" is determined by the process user ID. /proc files are accessible through standard system call interfaces: open, close, read, write, and ioctl. An open for reading and writing enables process control; a read-only open allows inspection but not control.

As with ordinary files, more than one process can open the same /proc file at the same time. Exclusive open is provided to allow controlling processes to avoid collisions; an open for writing that specifies O_EXCL fails if the file is already open for writing. If such an exclusive open succeeds, then subsequent attempts to open the file for writing, with or without the O_EXCL flag, fail until the exclusively opened file descriptor is closed. (Exception: a superuser open that does not specify O_EXCL succeeds even if the file is exclusively opened.) Any number of read-only opens are allowed, even when an exclusive write open is in effect on the file.

System Security

Except for a superuser, opening a /proc file fails unless both the user ID and group ID of the caller match those of the traced process and the process object file is readable by the caller. Files corresponding to setuid and setgid processes can be opened only by a superuser. Even if held by the superuser, an open process file descriptor becomes invalid if the traced process performs an exec of a setuid/setgid object file or an object file that it cannot read.

Any operation, except close, performed on an invalid file descriptor fails with the error EAGAIN. In this situation, if any tracing flags are set and the process file is open for writing, then the process will have been directed to stop, and its run-on-last-close flag will have been set (see PIOCSRLC). This protocol enables a controlling process (if it has permission) to reopen the process file to obtain a new valid file descriptor, close the invalid file descriptor, and proceed.

Just closing the invalid file descriptor causes the traced process to resume execution with no tracing flags set. A process that is not currently open for writing via /proc but which has left-over flags from a previous open and which then execs a setuid/setgid or unreadable object file will not be stopped, but will have all its tracing flags cleared.

Data Manipulation

Data can be transferred from or to any locations in the address space of the traced process. Use lseek to position the file at the virtual address of interest and follow it by read or write. You can apply the PIOCMAP operation to determine the accessible areas (mappings) of the address space. A contiguous area of the address space can appear as multiple mappings because of varying read/write/execute permissions. I/O transfers can span contiguous mappings. An I/O request extending into an unmapped area is truncated at the boundary.

Operations: Flags, Form, and Function

Process information and control operations involve the use of sets of flags. The set types sigset_t, fltset_t, and sysset_t correspond, respectively, to signal, fault, and system call enumerations defined in sys/signal.h, sys/fault.h, and sys/syscall.h. Each set type is large enough to hold flags for its own enumeration. Although they are of different sizes, they have a common structure and can be manipulated by the following macros.

```
prfillset(&set);                /* turn on all flags in set */
premptyset(&set);               /* turn off all flags in set */
praddset(&set, flag);           /* turn on the specified flag */
prdelset(&set flag);            /* turn off the specified flag* /
r = prismember(&set,flag);      /* != 0 iff flag is turned on */
```

One of prfillset or premptyset must be used to initialize set before it is used in any other operation. flag must be a member of the enumeration corresponding to set.

The operations have the form

```
#include <sys/types.h>
#include <sys/signal.h>
#include <sys/fault.h>
#include <sys/syscall.h>
#include <sys/procfs.h>
void *p;
retval = ioctl (fildes, code, p);
```

where

`sys/procfs.h`
: Contains definitions of `ioctl` codes and data structures used by the operations. Certain operations can be performed only if the process file is open for writing; these include all operations that affect process control.

The argument *p*
: A generic pointer whose type depends on the specific `ioctl` code. Where not specifically mentioned below, its value should be zero.

Information and control operations of `/proc` files are provided through `ioctl`. Each operation (`ioctl` or I/O) is guaranteed to be atomic with respect to the traced process, except when applied to a system process. More control operations than are strictly necessary are provided for efficiency and symmetry.

The allowable `ioctl` codes follow. Those operations requiring write access are marked with an asterisk (*). Except where noted, an `ioctl` to a process that has terminated elicits the error ENOENT.

Operations: Process Control

Processor control operations include the following categories.

- ▲ Stop and restart operations
- ▲ Signal traces
- ▲ Machine fault traces
- ▲ System call traces

- ▲ Register operations
- ▲ Memory mapping operations

Stop and Run Operations

The following operations stop a process or start it running again after a stop.

- PIOCSTOP*, PIOCWSTOP,
- PIOCRUN
- PIOCSRLC*, PIOCRRLC*

PIOCSTOP* and **PIOCWSTOP**

PIOCSTOP directs the process to stop and waits until it has stopped; PIOCWSTOP simply waits for the process to stop. These operations complete when the process stops on an event of interest, immediately if already so stopped. If *p* is non-zero, then it points to an instance of prstatus_t to be filled with status information for the stopped process.

An "event of interest" is either a PR_REQUESTED stop or a stop that has been specified in the process's tracing flags (set by PIOCSTRACE, PIOCSFAULT, PIOCSENTRY, and PIOCSEXIT). A PR_JOBCONTROL stop is specifically not an event of interest. (A process may stop twice because of a stop signal, first showing PR_SIGNALLED if the signal is traced and again showing PR_JOBCONTROL if the process is set running without clearing the signal.) If the process is controlled by ptrace, then it comes to a PR_SIGNALLED stop on receipt of any signal; this stop is an event of interest only if the signal is in the traced signal set. If PIOCSTOP is applied to a process that is stopped but not on an event of interest, then the stop directive takes effect when the process is restarted by the competing mechanism; at that time the process enters a PR_REQUESTED stop before executing any user-level code.

ioctls are interruptible by signals, so that, for example, an alarm can be set to avoid infinite waiting for a process that may never stop on an event of interest. If PIOCSTOP is interrupted, then the stop directive remains in effect even though the ioctl returns an error.

A system process (indicated by the PR_ISSYS flag) never executes at user level, has no user-level address space visible through /proc, and cannot be stopped. Applying PIOCSTOP or PIOCWSTOP to a system process elicits the error EBUSY.

PIOCRUN*

The traced process is made runnable again after a stop. PIOCRUN fails with EBUSY error if applied to a process that is not stopped on an event of interest. Once PIOCRUN has been applied, the process is no longer stopped on an event of interest even if, because of a competing mechanism, it remains stopped.

If *p* is non-zero, then it points to a prrun structure, shown in Figure 7-1, describing additional actions to be performed.

Figure 7-1
prrun Structure

```
typedef struct prrun {
  long      pr_flags;   /* Flags */
  sigset_t  pr_trace;   /* Set of signals to be traced */
  sigset_t  pr_sighold; /* Set of signals to be held */
  fltset_t  pr_fault;   /* Set of faults to be traced */
  caddr_t   pr_vaddr;   /* Virtual address at which to resume */
  long      pr_filler[8]; /* Filler area for future expansion */
} prrun_t;
```

pr_flags A bit mask describing optional actions, as listed in Table 7-1; the remainder of the entries are meaningful only if the appropriate bits are set in pr_flags.

Table 7-1 *pr_flags in PIOCRUN*

pr_flags	Meaning
PRCSIG	Clears the current signal, if any (see PIOCSSIG).
PRCFAULT	Clears the current fault, if any (see PIOCCFAULT).
PRSTRACE	Sets the traced signal set to pr_trace (see PIOCSTRACE).
PRSHOLD	Sets the held signal set to pr_sighold (see PIOCSHOLD).
PRSFAULT	Sets the trace fault set to pr_fault (see PIOCSFAULT).
PRSVADDR	Sets the address at which execution resumed to pr_vaddr .
PRSTEP	Directs the process to single-step; that is, to run and to execute a single machine instruction. On completion of the instruction, a hardware trace trap occurs. If FLTTRACE is being traced, then the process stops; otherwise, it is sent SIGTRAP. If SIGTRAP is being traced and not held, then the process stops. This operation requires hardware support and may not be implemented on all processors.

Table 7-1 *pr_flags in PIOCRUN (Continued)*

pr_flags	Meaning
PRSABORT	Instructs the process to abort execution of the system call (see PIOCSENTRY, PIOCSEXIT). Meaningful only if the process is in a PR_SYSENTRY stop or is marked PR_ASLEEP.
PRSTOP	Directs the process to stop again as soon as possible after resuming execution (see PIOCSTOP). In particular, if the process is stopped on PR_SIGNALLED or PR_FAULTED, then the next stop will show PR_REQUESTED, no other stop will have intervened, and the process will not have executed any user-level code.

pr_filler
: Reserved for future use; this area must be filled with zeros by your program.

PIOCSRLC* and **PIOCRRLC***

PIOCSRLC sets the run-on-last-close flag in the traced process: when the last writable /proc file descriptor referring to the traced process is closed, all of the process's tracing flags are cleared, any outstanding stop directive is canceled, and if the process is stopped, it is set running as though PIOCRUN had been applied to it. PIOCRRLC turns off the flag: the process's tracing flags are retained, and the process is not set running when the process file is closed.

Signal Operations

The following operations apply to signals as they affect a traced process.

- PIOCSTRACE*, PIOCGTRACE
- PIOCSSIG*
- PIOCKILL, PIOCUNKILL
- PIOCGHOLD, PIOCSHOLD*
- PIOCMAXSIG, PIOCACTION

PIOCSTRACE*

PIOCSTRACE defines a set of signals to be traced; the receipt of one of these signals causes the traced process to stop. The set of signals is defined via an instance of sigset_t addressed by *p*. Receipt of SIGKILL cannot be traced.

If a signal that is included in the held signal set is sent to the traced process, then the signal is not received. It does not cause a process stop until it is removed from the held signal set, either by the process itself or by setting the held signal set with PIOCSHOLD or the PRSHOLD option of PIOCRUN.

PIOCGTRACE

The current traced signal set is returned in an instance of sigset_t addressed by *p*.

PIOCSSIG*

The current signal and its associated signal information are set according to the contents of the siginfo structure addressed by *p* (see sys/siginfo.h). If the specified signal number is zero or if *p* is zero, then the current signal is cleared. The semantics of this operation are different from those of kill or PIOCKILL in that the signal is delivered to the process immediately after execution is resumed (even if it is being held) and an additional PR_SIGNALLED stop does not intervene even if the signal is traced. Setting the current signal to SIGKILL terminates the process immediately, even if it is stopped.

PIOCKILL*

A signal is sent to the process with semantics identical to those of kill; *p* points to an int naming the signal. Sending SIGKILL terminates the process immediately.

PIOCUNKILL*

A signal is deleted; that is, it is removed from the set of pending signals; the current signal (if any) is unaffected. *p* points to an int naming the signal. Attempting to delete SIGKILL results in an error.

PIOCGHOLD and **PIOCSHOLD***

PIOCGHOLD returns the set of held signals (signals whose delivery will be delayed if sent to the process) in an instance of sigset_t addressed by *p*. PIOCSHOLD correspondingly sets the held signal set but does not allow SIGKILL or SIGSTOP to be held.

PIOCMAXSIG and **PIOCACTION**

The operations provide information about the signal actions associated with the traced process [see sigaction(2)]. PIOCMAXSIG returns, in the int address by *p*, the maximum signal number understood by the system. This number can be used to allocate storage for use with the PIOCACTION operation, which returns the signal actions of the traced process in an array of sigaction structures addressed by *p*. Signal numbers are displaced by 1 from array indices, so that the action for signal number *n* appears in position *n*-1 of the array.

Machine Fault Operations

The following operations control the tracing of hardware faults.

- PIOCSFAULT*
- PIOCGFAULT, PIOCCFAULT*

PIOCSFAULT*

PIOCSFAULT defines a set of hardware faults to be traced. On incurring one of these faults, the traced process stops. The set is defined via an instance of fltset_t addressed by *p*. Fault names, defined in sys/fault.h, include the following. Some of the listed faults may not occur on all processors; in addition, processor-specific faults may occur.

FLTILL	Illegal instruction
FLTPRIV	Privileged instruction
FLTBPT	Breakpoint trap
FLTTRACE	Trace trap
FLTACCESS	Memory access fault
FLTBOUNDS	Memory bounds violation
FLTIOVF	Integer overflow
FLTIZDIV	Integer zero divide
FLTFPE	Floating-point exception
FLTSTACK	Unrecoverable stack fault
FLTPAGE	Recoverable page fault

When not traced, a fault normally results in the posting of a signal to the process that incurred the fault. If the process stops on a fault, then the signal is posted to the process when execution is resumed, unless the fault is cleared by PIOCCFAULT or by the PRCFAULT option of PIOCRUN. FLTPAGE is an exception: no signal is posted. Additional processor-specific faults can also be excepted in like manner. pr_info in the prstatus structure identifies the signal to be sent and contains machine-specific information about the fault.

PIOCGFAULT

The current traced fault set is returned in an instance of fltset_t addressed by *p*.

PIOCCFAULT

The current fault (if any) is cleared; the associated signal is not sent to the process.

System Call Operations

The following operations define the behavior of a process during system call tracing.

- PIOCSENTRY*, PIOCSEXIT*
- PIOCGENTRY, PIOCGEXIT
- PIOCSFORK*, PIOCRFORK*

PIOCSENTRY* and **PIOCSEXIT***

The operations instruct the process to stop on entry to or exit from specified system calls. The set of system calls to be traced is defined via an instance of sysset_t addressed by *p*.

When entry to a system call is being traced, the traced process stops after having begun the call to the system but before the system call arguments have been fetched from the process. When exit from a system call is being traced, the traced process stops on completion of the system call just prior to checking for signals and returning to user level. At this point, all return values have been stored into the traced process's saved registers.

If the traced process is stopped on entry to a system call (PR_SYSENTRY) or when sleeping in an interruptible system call (PR_ASLEEP is set), then it can be instructed to go directly to system call exit by specifying the PRSABORT flag in a PIOCRUN request. Unless exit from the system call is being traced, the process returns to user level showing error EINTR.

PIOCGENTRY and **PIOCGEXIT**

The operations return the current traced system call entry or exit set in an instance of sysset_t addressed by *p*.

PIOCSFORK* and **PIOCRFORK***

PIOCSFORK sets the inherit-on-fork flag in the traced process: the process's tracing flags are inherited by the child of a fork. PIOCRFORK turns off the flag; child processes start with all tracing flags cleared.

Register Operations

The following operations examine the saved register contents of a stopped process.

- PIOCGREG, PIOCSREG*
- PIOCGFPREG, PIOCSFPREG*

PIOCGREG and **PIOCSREG***
Respectively, the operations get and set the saved process registers into or out of an array addressed by *p*; the array has type gregset_t. Register contents are accessible via a set of predefined indices (see PIOCSTATUS). For security, certain bits of the processor-status word cannot be modified by PIOCSREG. There may be other privileged registers that cannot be modified at all. PIOCSREG fails with EBUSY error if applied to a process that is not stopped on an event of interest.

PIOCGFPREG and **PIOCSFPREG***
Respectively, the operations get and set the saved process floating-point registers into or out of a structure addressed by *p*; the structure has type fpregset_t. If the machine has no floating-point hardware, then the error EINVAL is returned. PIOCSFPREG fails (EBUSY) if applied to a process that is not stopped on an event of interest.

Memory Mapping Operations

The following operations locate the virtual address of a traced process or mapped object associated with a traced object.

- PIOCNMAP, PIOCMAP
- PIOCOPENM

PIOCNMAP and **PIOCMAP**
The operations provide information about the memory mappings (virtual address ranges) associated with the traced process. PIOCNMAP returns, in the int addressed by *p*, the number of mappings that are currently active. The number can be used to allocate storage for use with the PIOCMAP operation, which returns the list of currently active mappings. For PIOCMAP, *p* addresses an array of elements of type prmap_t; one array element (one structure) is returned for each mapping, plus an additional

element containing all zeros to mark the end of the list. Figure 7-2 shows the prmap structure.

Figure 7-2 *prmap Structure*

```
typedef struct prmap {
  caddr_t   pr_vaddr;   /* Virtual address base */
  u_long    pr_size;    /* Size of mapping in bytes */
  off_t     pr_off;     /* Offset into mapped object,if any */
  long      pr_mflags;  /* Protection and attribute flags */
  long      pr_filler[4];/* Filler for future expansion */
) prmap_t;
```

The members have the following meaning.

pr_vaddr The virtual address base (the lower limit) of the mapping within the traced process.

pr_size The size in bytes of the mapping within the traced process.

pr_off The offset within the mapped object (if any) to which the address base is mapped.

pr_mflags
A bit-mask of protection and attribute flags, as listed below.

Table 7-2 *pr_mflags in PIOCNMAP and PIOCMAP*

pr_mflags	Meaning
MA_READ	Mapping is readable by the traced process.
MA_WRITE	Mapping is writable by the traced process.
MA_EXEC	Mapping is executable by the traced process.
MA_SHARED	Mapping changes are shared by the mapped object.
MA_BREAK	Mapping is grown by the brk system call.
MA_STACK	Mapping is grown automatically on stack faults.

PIOCOPENM
The return value *retval* provides a read-only file descriptor for a mapped object associated with the traced process. If *p* is zero, then the traced process's `exec`ed file (its `a.out` file) is found. This value enables a debugger to find the object file symbol table without having to know the path name of the executable file. If *p* is non-zero, then it points to a `caddr_t` containing a virtual address within the traced process and the mapped object (if any) associated with that address is found; the address can be used to obtain a file descriptor for a shared library that is attached to the process. On error (invalid address or no mapped object for the designated address), `-1` is returned.

Operations: Process Information

Process information operations include the following categories.

- ▲ Process status or miscellaneous information
- ▲ Process identification, such as credentials, group IDs, and so forth

Process Status or Information Operations

The following operations return status or other information for a process or allow you to alter priority status.

- PIOCSTATUS
- PIOCNICE
- PIOCPSINFO

PIOCSTATUS
The operation returns status information for a process; *p* is a pointer to a `prstatus` structure, which is shown in Figure 7-3.

Figure 7-3
***prstatus* Structure**

```
typedef struct prstatus {
  long       pr_flags;    /* Process flags */
  short      pr_why;      /* Reason for process stop (if stopped) */
  short      pr_what;     /* More detailed reason */
  struct siginfo pr_info; /* Info associated with signal or fault */
  short      pr_cursig;   /*Current signal */
  sigset_t   pr_sigpend;  /* Set of other pending signals */
  sigset_t   pr_sighold;  /* Set of held signals */
  struct sigalstack pr_altstack; /* Alternate signal stack info */
  struct sigaction pr_action; /* Signal action for current signal */
  pid_t      pr_pid;      /* Process ID */
  pid_t      pr_ppid;     /* Parent process ID */
  pid_t      pr_pgrp;     /* Process group ID */
  pid_t      pr_sid;      /* Session ID */
  timestruc_t pr_utime;/* Process user CPU time */
  timestruc_t pr_stime;/* Process system CPU time */
  timestruc_t pr_cutime;/* Sum of children's user times */
  timestruc_t pr_cstime;/* Sum of children's system times */
  char       pr_clname[8];/* Scheduling class name */
  long       pr_filler[20];/* Filler area for future expansion */
  long       pr_instr;    /* Current instruction */
  gregset_t pr_reg;       /* General registers */
} prstatus_t;
```

The members have the following meaning.

`pr_flags` A bit-mask holding the flags listed in Table 7-3.

Table 7-3 *pr_flags in PIOCSTATUS*

pr_flag	**Meaning**
PR_STOPPED	Process is stopped.
PR_ISTOP	Process is stopped on an event of interest (see PIOCSTOP).
PR_DSTOP	Process has a stop directive in effect (see PIOCSTOP).
PR_ASLEEP	Process is in an interruptible sleep within a system call.
PR_FORK	Process has its inherit-on-fork flag set (see PIOCSFORK).
PR_RLC	Process has its run-on-last-close flag set (see PIOCSRLC).
PR_PTRACE	Process is being traced via ptrace.

Table 7-3 *pr_flags in PIOCSTATUS (Continued)*

pr_flag	Meaning
PR_PCINVAL	Process program counter refers to an invalid address.
PR_ISSYS	Process is a system process (see PIOCSTOP).

pr_why and pr_what

For a stopped process, describe the reason that the process is stopped. Possible values of pr_why and corresponding pr_what values are listed in Table 7-4.

Table 7-4 *Values of pr_why and pr_what*

pr_why	Meaning	Corresponding pr_what Values
PR_REQUESTED	Process stopped because PIOCSTOP was applied.	Unused.
PR_SIGNALLED	Process stopped on receipt of a signal (see PIOCSTRACE).	Holds the signal number that caused the stop; for a newly-stopped process, the same value is in pr_cursig.
PR_FAULTED	Process stopped on incurring a hardware fault (see PIOCSFAULT).	Holds the fault number that caused the stop.
PR_SYSENTRY PR_SYSEXIT	Indicates a stop on entry to or exit from a system call (see PIOCSENTRY and PIOCSEXIT).	Holds the system call number.
PR_JOBCONTROL	Indicates that the process stopped because of the default action of a job control stop signal (see sigaction).	Holds the stopping signal number.

pr_info When the process is in a PR_SIGNALLED or PR_FAULTED stop, contains additional information pertinent to the particular signal or fault (see sys/siginfo.h).

pr_cursig, pr_sigpend, and pr_sighold

pr_cursig names the current signal; that is, the next signal to be delivered to the process. pr_sigpend identifies other pending signals. pr_sighold identifies those signals whose delivery is being delayed if sent to the process.

pr_altstack and pr_action
: pr_altstack contains the alternate signal stack information for the process (see sigalstack). pr_action contains the signal action information pertaining to the current signal (see sigaction); if pr_cursig is zero, then pr_action is undefined.

pr_pid, pr_ppid, pr_pgrp, and pr_sid
: Respectively, the process ID, the ID of the process's parent, the process's process group ID, and the process's session ID.

pr_utime, pr_stime, pr_cutime, and pr_cstime
: Respectively, the user CPU and system CPU time consumed by the process and the cumulative user CPU and system CPU time consumed by the process's children, in seconds and nanoseconds.

pr_clname
: Contains the name of the scheduling class of the process.

pr_filler
: Reserved for future use.

pr_instr Contains the machine instruction to which the program counter refers. The amount of data retrieved from the process is machine-dependent. In general, the size is that of the machine's smallest instruction. If the program counter refers to an invalid address, then PR_PCINVAL is set, and pr_instr is undefined.

pr_reg An array holding the contents of the general registers. The constants defined in sys/regset.h can be used as indices to refer to the general registers.

PIOCNICE*

The traced process's nice priority is incremented by the amount contained in the int addressed by *p*. Only a superuser can better a process's priority in this way, but any user can lower the priority.

PIOCPSINFO

PIOCPSINFO returns miscellaneous process information such as that reported by ps(1). *p* is a pointer to a prpsinfo structure, shown in Figure 7-4, containing at least the following fields.

Figure 7-4 ***prpsinfo* Structure**

```
typedef struct prpsinfo {
  char     pr_state;     /* Numeric process state (see pr_name) */
  char     pr_sname;     /* Printable character representing pr_state
*/
  char     pr_zomb;      /* !=0; process terminated but not waited for
*/
  char     pr_nice;      /* nice for cpu usage */
  u_long   pr_flag;      /* Process flags */
  uid_t    pr_uid;       /* Real user ID */
  gid_t    pr_gid;       /* Real group ID */
  pid_t    pr_pid;       /* Unique process ID */
  pid_t    pr_ppid       /* Process ID of parent */
  pid_t    pr_pgrp;      /* pid of process group leader */
  pid_t    pr_sid;       /* Session ID */
  caddr_t  pr_addr;      /* Physical address of process */
  long     pr_size       /* Size of process image in pages */
  long     pr_rssize;    /* Resident set size in pages */
  caddr_t  pr_wchan;     /* Wait addr for sleeping process */
  timestruc_t pr_start   /* Process start time, sec+nsec since epoch
*/
  timestruc_t pr_time;   /* usr+sys CPU time for this process */
  long     pr_pri;       /* Priority, high value is high priority */
  char     pr_oldpri;    /* Pre-SVR4, low value is high priority */
  char     pr_cpu        /* Pre-SVR4, cpu usage for scheduling */
  dev_t    pr_ttydev;    /* Controlling tty device (PRNODEV if none)
*/
  char     pr_clname[8] /* Scheduling class name */
  char     pr_fname[16] /* Last component of execed pathname */
  char     pr_psargs[PRARGSZ] /* Initial characters of arg list */
  long     pr_filler[20]/* For future expansion */
} prpsinfo_t;
```

Some of the entries in prpsinfo, such as pr_state and pr_flag, are system-specific and should not be expected to retain their meanings across different versions of the operating system. pr_addr is a vestige of the past with no real meaning in current systems.

PIOCPSINFO can be applied to a zombie process (one that has terminated but whose parent has not yet performed a wait on it).

Process Identification Operations

The following operations identify various process parameters.

- PIOCCRED
- PIOCGROUPS
- PIOCGETPR, PIOCGETU

PIOCCRED

PIOCCRED fetches the set of credentials associated with the process. *p* points to an instance of prcred_t, which is filled by the following operation. Figure 7-5 shows the prcred structure.

Figure 7-5
prcred Structure

```
typedef struct prcred {
  uid_t     pr_euid;     /* Effective user ID */
  uid_t     pr_ruid;     /* Real user ID */
  uid_t     pr_suide;    /* Saved user ID (from exec) */
  uid_t     pr_egid;     /* Effective group ID */
  uid_t     pr_rgid;     /* Real group ID */
  uid_t     pr_sgid;     /* Saved group ID (from exec) */
  uid_t     pr_ngroups; /* Number of supplementary groups */
} prcred_t;
```

PIOCGROUPS

PIOCGROUPS fetches the set of supplementary group IDs associated with the process. *p* points to an array of elements of type uid_t, which will be filled by the operation. PIOCCRED can be applied beforehand to determine the number of groups (pr_ngroups) that will be returned and the amount of storage that should be allocated to hold them.

PIOCGETPR and **PIOCGETU**

The operations copy, respectively, the traced process's group proc structure and user area into the buffer addressed by *p*. They are provided for completeness, but it should be unnecessary to access either of these structures directly, because relevant status information is available through other control operations. Their use is discouraged because a program making use of them is tied to a particular version of the operating system.

PIOCGETPR is applicable to a zombie process (see PIOCPSINFO on page 179).

Error Messages Associated with `/proc`

Errors that can occur, in addition to the errors normally associated with file system access, are described below.

`ENOENT` The traced process has exited after being opened.

`EIO` I/O was attempted at an illegal address in the traced process.

`EBADF` An I/O or `ioctl` operation requiring write access was attempted on a file descriptor not open for writing.

`EBUSY` `PIOCSTOP` or `PIOCWSTOP` was applied to a system process; an exclusive `open` was attempted on a process already open for writing; an `open` for writing was attempted and an exclusive `open` is in effect on the process file. `PIOCRUN`, `PIOCSREG`, or `PIOCSFPREG` was applied to a process not stopped on an event of interest; an attempt was made to mount `/proc` when it is already mounted.

`EPERM` Someone other than superuser attempted to better a process's priority by issuing `PIOCNICE`.

`ENOSYS` An attempt was made to perform an unsupported operation (such as create, remove, link, or unlink) on an entry in `/proc`.

`EFAULT` An I/O or `ioctl` request referred to an invalid address in the controlling process.

`EINVAL` In general, an invalid argument was supplied to a system call. The list of conditions eliciting the error includes the following:

- The `ioctl` code is undefined
- An `ioctl` operation was issued on a file descriptor referring to the `/proc` directory
- An out-of-range signal number was specified with `PIOCSSIG`, `PIOCKILL`, or `PIOCUNKILL`
- `SIGKILL` was specified with `PIOCUNKILL`

- An illegal virtual address was specified in a `PIOCOPENM` request
- `PIOCGFPREG` or `PIOCSFPREG` was issued on a machine without floating-point hardware

`EINTR` A signal was received by the controlling process while it waited for the traced process to stop via `PIOCSTOP` or `PIOCWSTOP`.

`EAGAIN` The traced process has performed an `exec` of a setuid/setgid object file or of an object file that it cannot read; all further operations on the process file descriptor (except `close`) elicit this error.

❑ Process Traces through `truss`

`truss`(1) is a new command (written using the `/proc` facilities described above) that will produce a symbolic trace of the activity of a running process: system calls executed, and signals or machine faults incurred. It can be used to start up a command and trace its activity or it can be applied to an already running process. Each line of the trace output reports either the fault or signal name or the system call name with its arguments and return value(s). System call arguments are displayed symbolically when possible, using defines from relevant system header files; for any path name pointer argument, the pointed-to string is displayed.

Every machine fault (except a page fault) results in the posting of a signal to the process that incurred the fault. A report of a received signal immediately follows each report of a machine fault (except a page fault) unless that signal is being blocked by the process.

Error returns are reported according to the error code names described in Appendix A.

`truss` *Constraints*

This section provides information about `truss` that may be non-standard or not obvious.

- The operating system enforces certain security restrictions on the trace of processes. In particular, any command whose object file (`a.out`) cannot be read by a user cannot be traced by that user; `set-uid` and `set-gid` commands can be traced only by a privileged user. Unless it is run by a privileged user, `truss` loses control of any process that performs an `exec`(2) of a `set-id` or unreadable object file; such processes continue normally, though independently of `truss`, from the point of the `exec`.
- To avoid collisions with other controlling processes, `truss` does not trace a process which it detects is being controlled by another process via the `/proc` interface. This protections allows `truss` to be applied to `proc`-based debuggers as well as to another instance of itself.
- The system may run out of per-user process slots when tracing of children is requested. When tracing more than one process, `truss` runs as one controlling process for each process being traced. (See the `spell` example on page 187.)
- `truss` uses shared memory and semaphores when dealing with more than one process, as when the `-f` option is specified or when the `-p` option with more than one `pid` is specified. When these entities are needed but not configured in the system, `truss` issues a warning message and proceeds. However, the trace output may become garbled in this case; the output of the `-c` option reports only the top-level command or first `pid`, and no children are counted.
- The trace output for multiple processes is not produced in strict time order. For example, a `read` on a pipe may be reported before the corresponding `write`. For any one process, the output is strictly time-ordered.
- Be aware that some system calls described in section 2 manual pages differ from actual operating system interfaces; trace output may deviate slightly from the section 2 descriptions.

`truss` *Options*

`truss` options allow you to trace, or exclude from tracing, specified or all system calls, signals, machine faults for a process or list of existing processes. You can control characteristics of the trace output, including traces of children created by `fork`. You can examine the I/O buffer for `read/write` on file descriptors.

The `truss` command has the form

`truss` [`-p`] [`-f`] [`-c`] [`-a`] [`-e`] [`-i`] [`-`[`tvx`] [`!`] *syscall* . . .] \
[`-s`[`!`] *signal* . . .] [`-m`[`!`]*fault* . . .] [`-`[`rw`] [`!`]*fd* . . .] [`-o` *outfile*]\
command

For options that take a list argument,

- you can use the name `all` to specify all possible members of a list.
- you can use `!` at the beginning of a list to reverse the meaning of an option; for example, to exclude, rather than trace, listed members.
- you can specify multiple occurrences of the same option. If the same name appears more than once in a list, then subsequent options (those to the right) override previous ones (those to the left).

Input/Output Options

You can use the `-p` option to `truss` to specify a list of process IDs. `truss` interprets the argument as a list of existing processes [see `ps`(1)] rather than as a command to be executed. When `-p` is specified, `truss` takes control of each process and begins tracing it, provided that a) the userid and groupid of the process match those of the user or b) that the user is a privileged user. You can also specify processes by their names in the /proc directory (even remotely mounted `/proc` directories); for example, `/proc/1234`.

By default, the trace output of truss goes to standard error. However, you can specify, by means of the `-o` option, a file to be used instead. Use of the `-o` option also provides two interesting possibilities.

- You can facilitate tracing of interactive programs which catch interrupt and quit signals from the terminal.

  That is, if you use `truss` to initiate and trace a specified command and if you also specify the `-o` option or redirect standard error to a non-terminal file, then `truss` runs with hangup, interrupt, and quit signals ignored.
- You can terminate excessive trace output and release previously existing processes. Released processes continue normally, as if they had never been touched.

If the trace output remains directed to the terminal or if existing processes are traced (as happens when the `-p` option is specified), then `truss` responds to hangup, interrupt, and quit signals by releasing all traced processes and exiting.

Inclusive Options

To follow all children created by `fork` and include their signals, faults, and system calls in the trace output, use the `-f` option to `truss`. When you specify `-f`, the process ID is included with each line of trace output to show which process executed the system call or received the signal.

◆ ***Note:*** Normally, only the first-level command or process is traced.

To count traced system calls, faults, and signals rather than display the trace line-by-line, use the `-c` option to `truss`. A summary report is produced after the traced command terminates or when `truss` is interrupted. If you also specify `-f`, then the counts include all traced system calls, faults, and signals for child processes.

Signal Options

To trace specified signals, use the `-s` option to `truss`. You can specify signals by name or number (see `sys/signal.h`), or you can accept the option default (`-sall`) to include all signals. To exclude signals from the trace output, precede the list with `!` (exclamation point).

The trace output reports the receipt of each specified signal, even if the signal is being ignored (not blocked) by the process.

◆ ***Note:*** Blocked signals are not received until the process releases them.

Other options that report signal information are `-f` (traces children processes) and `-c` (includes in summary count).

Machine Fault Options

To trace specified machine faults, use the -m option (-m[!] *fault*,...) to truss. You can specify faults by name or number (see sys/fault.h). The option default is -mall -m!fltpage. To exclude faults from the trace output, precede the list with !.

Other options that report fault information are -f (traces children processes) and -c (includes in summary count).

System Call Options

truss provides several options that allow you to particularize system call traces. That is,

- You can specify, by means of the -t option, a list of system calls to be traced or you can accept the default (-tall) to trace all system calls. To exclude system calls from the trace output, precede the list with !.
- If you are an unredeemed hacker, you can use the -x option to display the arguments to the specified system calls (if traced) in raw form, usually hexadecimal, rather than symbolically. Or, you can accept the default, -x!all.
- You can display, by means of the -v option, the contents of structures passed by address to the specified system calls (if traced). The -v (for verbose) option shows input values and values returned by the operating system. If a field is used as both input and output, then only the output value is shown.

◆ ***Note:*** Not all possible structures passed in all possible system calls are displayed.

- You can use the -a option to show the argument strings passed in each exec system call.
- You can use the -e option to show the environment strings passed in each exec system call.
- You can inhibit display of interruptible sleeping system calls by specifying the -i option.

  Certain system calls, such as open and read on terminal devices or pipes can sleep for indefinite periods and are interruptible. Normally, `truss` reports such sleeping system calls if they remain asleep for more than one second; the system call is reported again a second time when it completes. The `-i` option causes such system calls to be reported only once, when they complete.

File Descriptor Options

Two options to truss, `-r` and `-w`, show the full contents of the I/O buffer for each `read` or `write`, respectively, on any specified file descriptor. The output is formatted 32 bytes per line.

The output shows each byte as an ASCII character (preceded by one blank) or as a two-character C language escape sequence for control characters, such as horizontal tab (\t) and newline (\n). If ASCII interpretation is not possible, then the byte is shown in two-character hexadecimal representation.

◆ ***Note:*** The first 16 bytes of the I/O buffer for each traced read are shown even in the absence of `-r`.

`truss` Examples

The following examples illustrate the results of using `truss` with various options.

▲ This example produces a trace of the `find`(1) command on the terminal:

```
truss find . -print >find.out
```

▲ This example produces a trace of only the `open`, `close`, `read`, and `write` system calls:

```
truss -t open,close,read,write find . -print >find.out
```

▲ This command produces a trace of the `spell`(1) command on the file `truss.out`:

```
truss -f -o truss.out spell document
```

`spell` is a shell script, so the `-f` flag is needed to trace not only the shell but also the processes created by the shell. This example illustrates how process slots can exceed the allowable per-user number. `spell` itself uses 9 process slots, 1 for the shell and 8 for the eight-member pipeline, while `truss` adds another 9 processes, for a total of 18. This number is perilously close to the usual system-imposed limit of 25 processes per user.

▲ This command produces a tiresome output (97% of the output) of `lseek`, `read`, and `write` system calls:

```
truss nroff -mm document >nroff.out
```

To abbreviate the report, the command is:

```
truss -t !lseek,read,write nroff -mm document >nroff.out
```

▲ This example verbosely traces the activity of process #1, `init`(1M) and assumes that the command is issued by a privileged user. Interrupting `truss` returns `init` to normal operation.

```
truss -p -v all 1
```

A

System Call Error Returns

Most system calls have one or more error returns. An error condition is indicated by an otherwise impossible returned value. This value is almost always `-1` or the `NULL` pointer; the individual descriptions specify the details. An error number is also made available in the external variable `errno`. `errno` is not cleared on successful calls, so it should be tested only after an error has been indicated.

The constants `ARG_MAX`, `SYS_OPEN`, `OPEN_MAX`, and so forth are implementation-specified constants defined in `limits.h`. See `limits`(4).

Each system call description attempts to list all possible error numbers. Table A-1 is a complete list of error number and their names, as defined in `errno.h`.

Table A-1 *System Call Errors*

No.	name summary	Meaning
1	EPERM Not privileged	Typically, the error indicates an attempt to modify a file in some way forbidden by the privilege mechanism or restricted to the owner of the file. Also returned when an attempt is made to open a device already open by another process.
2	ENOENT No such file or directory	A file name is specified and the file should exist but does not, or one of the directories in a path name does not exist.
3	ESRCH No such process	No process can be found corresponding to the process identifier specified.
4	EINTR Interrupted system call	An asynchronous signal (such as interrupt or quit), which the user has elected to catch, occurred during a system service routine. If execution is resumed after processing the signal, it will appear as if the interrupted routine call returned this error condition.
5	EIO I/O error	Some physical I/O error has occurred. The error may in some cases occur on a call following the one to which it actually applies.
6	ENXIO No such device or address	I/O on a special file refers to a subdevice which does not exist, or exists beyond the limit of the device. It may also occur when, for example, a tape drive is not on-line or no disk pack is loaded on a drive.
7	E2BIG Arg list too long	An argument list longer than ARG_MAX bytes is presented to a member of the exec family of routines. The argument list limit is the sum of the size of the argument list plus the size of the environment's exported shell variables.
8	ENOEXEC Exec format error	A request is made to execute a file which, although it has the appropriate permissions, does not start with a valid format [see a.out on page 7].
9	EBADF Bad file number	Either a file descriptor refers to no open file, or a read (respectively, write) request is made to a file that is open only for writing (respectively, reading).
10	ECHILD No child process	A wait routine was executed by a process that had no existing or unwaited-for child process.

Table A-1 *System Call Errors (Continued)*

No.	name summary	Meaning
11	`EAGAIN` Resource is temporarily unavailable; try again later	For example, a `fork` routine failed because the system's process table is full or the user is not allowed to create any more processes; or a system call failed because of insufficient memory or swap space.
12	`ENOMEM` Not enough space	During execution of an `exec`, `brk`, or `sbrk` routine, a program asks for more space than the system is able to supply. This is not a temporary condition; the maximum size is a system parameter. The error may also occur if the arrangement of text, data, and stack segments requires too many segmentation registers, or if there is not enough swap space during the `fork` routine. If the error occurs on a resource associated with Remote File Sharing (RFS), it indicates a memory depletion which may be temporary, depending on system activity at the time the call was invoked.
13	`EACCES` Permission denied	An attempt was made to access a file in a way forbidden by the protection system. The access control mechanism grants and denies a process permission to access an object based on a comparison of the attributes of the process (real and effective user IDs) and the attributes of the object (access permissions). Failure of any of these checks causes denial of the requested access and the return of `EACCES`.
14	`EFAULT` Bad address	The system encountered a hardware fault in attempting to use an argument of a routine. For example, `errno` potentially may be set to `EFAULT` whenever a routine that takes a pointer argument is passed an invalid address, if the system can detect the condition. Because systems differ in their ability to reliably detect a bad address, on some implementations passing a bad address to a routine results in undefined behavior.
15	`ENOTBLK` Block device required	A non-block file was mentioned where a block device was required; for example, in a call to the `mount` routine.
16	`EBUSY` Device busy	The device or resource is currently unavailable. An attempt was made to do one of the following: mount a device that was already mounted; unmount a device on which there is an active file (open file, current directory, mounted-on file, active text segment); enable accounting when it is already enabled; or, open a device that is in the process of closing.

Table A-1 *System Call Errors (Continued)*

No.	name summary	Meaning
17	EEXIST File exists	An existing file was mentioned in an inappropriate context; for example, call to the link routine.
18	EXDEV Cross-device link	A link to a file on another device was attempted.
19	ENODEV No such device	An attempt was made to apply an inappropriate operation to a device; for example, read a write-only device, open a device not yet allocated.
20	ENOTDIR Not a directory	A non-directory was specified where a directory is required; for example, in a path prefix or as an argument to the chdir routine.
21	EISDIR Is a directory	An attempt was made to perform an operation not appropriate for a directory, such as write(2).
22	EINVAL Invalid argument	An invalid argument was specified; for example, unmounting a non-mounted device or specifying an undefined signal in a call to sigaction(2) or kill(2).
23	ENFILE File table overflow	The system file table is full; that is, SYS_OPEN files are open, and temporarily no more files can be opened.
24	EMFILE Too many open files	No process can have more than OPEN_MAX file descriptors open at a time.
25	ENOTTY Not a typewriter	A call was made to the ioctl routine specifying a file that is not a special character device.
26	ETXTBSY Text file busy	An attempt was made to execute a pure-procedure program that is currently open for writing. Also, an attempt to open for writing or to remove a pure-procedure program that is being executed.
27	EFBIG File too large	The size of a file exceeded the maximum file size, FCHR_MAX (see getrlimit).
28	ENOSPC No space left on device	While writing an ordinary file or creating a directory entry, no free space is left on the device. In the fcntl routine, the setting or removing of record locks on a file cannot be accomplished because no more record entries are left on the system.
29	ESPIPE Illegal seek	A call to the lseek routine was issued to a pipe.

Table A-1 *System Call Errors (Continued)*

No.	name summary	Meaning
30	EROFS Read-only file system	An attempt to modify a file or directory was made on a file system which was mounted read-only.
31	EMLINK Too many links	An attempt was made to make more than the maximum number of links, LINK_MAX, to a file.
32	EPIPE Broken pipe	A write on a pipe for which there is no process to read the data. This condition normally generates a signal; the error is returned if the signal is ignored.
33	EDOM Math argument out of domain of func	The argument of a function in the math package (3M) is out of the domain of the function.
34	ERANGE Math result not representable	The value of a function in the math package (3M) is not representable within machine precision.
35	ENOMSG No message of desired type	An attempt was made to receive a message of a type that does not exist on the specified message queue [see msgop(2)].
36	EIDRM Identifier removed	The error is returned to processes that resume execution because of removal of a message or semaphore identifier from the system [see magop(2), semop(2), msgctl(2), and semctl(2)].
37	ECHRNG	Channel number is out of range.
38	EL2NSYNC	Level 2 is not synchronized.
39	EL3HLT	Level 3 is halted.
40	EL3RST	Level 3 is reset.
41	ELNRNG	Link number is out of range.
42	EUNATCH	Protocol driver not attached.
43	ENOCSI	No CSI structure is available.
44	EL2HLT	Level 2 is halted.
45	EDEADLK Deadlock condition	A deadlock situation was detected and avoided. The error pertains to file and record locking.

Table A-1 *System Call Errors (Continued)*

No.	name summary	Meaning
46	`ENOLCK` No record locks available	No more locks are available. The system lock table is full [see `fcntl`(2)].
47-49	Reserved	
58-59	Reserved	
60	`ENOSTR` Device not a stream	A `putmsg` or `getmsg` system call was attempted on a file descriptor that is not a STREAMS device.
61	`ENODATA`	No data are available.
62	`ETIME` Timer expired	The timer set for a STREAMS `ioctl` call has expired. The cause of the error is device specific and could indicate either a hardware or software failure, or perhaps a timeout value that is too short for the specific operation. The status of the `ioctl` operation is indeterminate.
63	`ENOSR` Out of stream resources	During a STREAMS `open`, either no STREAMS queues or no STREAMS head data structures were available. The condition is temporary; one may recover from it if other processes release resources.
64	`ENONET` Machine is not on the network	The error is Remote File Sharing (RFS) specific. It occurs when users try to advertise, unadvertise, mount, or unmount remote resources while the machine has not done the proper startup to connect to the network.
65	`ENOPKG` Package not installed	The error occurs when users attempt to use a system call from a package that has not been installed.
66	`EREMOTE` Object is remote	The error is RFS specific. It occurs when users try to advertise a resource that is not on the local machine or try to mount/unmount a device (or path name) that is on a remote machine.
67	`ENOLINK` Link severed	The error is RFS specific. It occurs when the link (virtual circuit) connecting to a remote machine is gone.
68	`EADV` Advertise error	The error is RFS specific. It occurs when users try to advertise a resource that has already been advertised, try to stop RFS while resources are still advertised, or try to force-unmount a resource when it is still advertised.

Table A-1 *System Call Errors (Continued)*

No.	name summary	Meaning
69	ESRMNT Srmount error	The error is RFS specific. It occurs when an attempt is made to stop RFS while resources are still mounted by remote machines, or when a resource is readvertised with a client list that does not include a remote machine that currently has the resource mounted.
70	ECOMM Communication error on send	The error is RFS specific. It occurs when the current process is waiting for a message from a remote machine and the virtual circuit fails.
71	EPROTO Protocol error	A protocol error occurred. The error is device specific, but is generally not related to a hardware failure.
74	EMULTIHOP Multihop attempted	The error is RFS specific. It occurs when users try to access remote resources that are not directly accessible.
76	EDOTDOT	The error is RFS specific. It is a way for the server to tell the client that a process has transferred back from mount point.
77	EBADMSG Not a data message	During a `read`, `getmsg`, or `ioctl I_RECVFD` system call to a STREAMS device, something has come to the head of the queue that cannot be processed. That something depends on the system call: `read` control information or a passed file descriptor `getmsg` passed file descriptor `ioctl` control or data information
78	ENAMETOOLONG File name too long	The length of the path argument exceeds `PATH_MAX`, or the length or a path component exceeds `NAME_MAX` while `_POSIX_NO_TRUNC` is in effect [see `limits`(4)].
79	EOVERFLOW	Value is too large for the defined data type.
80	ENOTUNIQ Name not unique on network	The given log name is not unique.
81	EBADFD File descriptor in bad state	Either a file descriptor refers to no open file, or a read request was made to a file that is open only for writing.
82	EREMCHG	Remote address is changed.
83	ELIBACC Cannot access a needed shared library	An operation tried to `exec` an `a.out` that requires a static shared library and the shared library does not exist or the user does not have permission to use it.

Table A-1 *System Call Errors (Continued)*

No.	name summary	Meaning
84	ELIBBAD Accessing a corrupted shared library	An operation tried to exec an a.out that requires a static shared library (to be linked in) and exec could not load the static shared library. The static shared library is probably corrupted.
85	ELIBSCN .lib section in a.out corrupted	An operation tried to exec an a.out that requires a static shared library (to be linked in) and erroneous data were in the .lib section of a.out. The .lib section tells exec the static shared libraries that are needed. The a.out is probably corrupted.
86	ELIBMAX Trying to link in more shared libraries than system limit	An operation tried to exec an a.out that requires more static shared libraries than are allowed on the current configuration of the system.
87	ELIBEXEC Cannot exec a shared library	An operation attempted to exec a shared library directly.
88	EILSEQ	Illegal byte sequence was encountered; handle multiple characters as a single character.
89	ENOSYS	Operation is not applicable.
90	ELOOP	Too many symbolic links are in path name traversal.
91	ESTART Restartable system call	Interrupted system call should be restarted.
92	ESTRPIPE Streams pipe error	Streams pipe error occurred (not externally visible).
93	ENOTEMPTY	The directory was not empty.
94	EUSERS	There are too many users.
95	ENOTSOCK	A socket operation was attempted on non-socket.
96	EDESTADDRREQ Destination address required	A required address was omitted from an operation on a transport endpoint. A destination address is required.
97	EMSGSIZE Message too long	A message sent on a transport provider was larger than the internal message buffer or some other network limit.

Table A-1 *System Call Errors (Continued)*

No.	name summary	Meaning
98	EPROTOTYPE Protocol wrong type for socket	A specified protocol does not support the semantics of the socket type requested.
99	ENOPROTOOPT Protocol not available	A bad option or level was specified when getting or setting options for a protocol.
120	EPROTONOSUPPORT Protocol not supported	The protocol has not been configured into the system or no implementation for it exists.
121	ESOCKTNOSUPPORT Socket type not supported	The support for the socket type has not been configured into the system or no implementation for it exists.
122	EOPNOTSUPP	The operation is not supported on transport endpoint; for example, trying to accept a connection on a datagram transport endpoint.
123	EPFNOSUPPORT Protocol family not supported	The protocol family has not been configured into the system or no implementation for it exists. Used for the Internet protocols.
124	EAFNOSUPPORT Address family not supported by protocol family	An address incompatible with the requested protocol was used.
125	EADDRINUSE Address already in use	User attempted to use an address already in use, and the protocol does not allow such usage.
126	EADDRNOTAVAIL Cannot assign requested address	An attempt was made to create a transport endpoint with an address not on the current machine.
127	ENETDOWN Network down	The operation encountered a dead network.
128	ENETUNREACH Network unreachable	The operation was attempted to an unreachable network.

Table A-1 *System Call Errors (Continued)*

No.	name summary	Meaning
129	`ENETRESET` Network dropped connection because of reset	The host to which a user was connected crashed and rebooted.
130	`ECONNABORTED` Software caused connection abort	A connection abort was caused internal to user's host machine.
131	`ECONNRESET` Connection reset by peer	A connection was forcibly closed by a peer. This error normally results from a loss of the connection on the remote host because of a timeout or a reboot.
132	`ENOBUFS` No buffer space available	An operation on a transport endpoint or pipe was not performed because the system lacked sufficient buffer space or because a queue was full.
133	`EISCONN` Transport endpoint already connected	A connect request was made on an already connected transport endpoint, or a `sendto` or `sendmsg` request on a connected transport endpoint specified a destination when already connected.
134	`ENOTCONN` Transport endpoint not connected	A request to send or receive data was disallowed because the transport endpoint is not connected and (when sending a datagram) no address was supplied.
137	`ENOTNAM` Not a XENIX system named type file	A XENIX system "named" file (semaphore, shared data, and so forth) was expected, but the specified object was not a XENIX system named file.
138	`ENAVAIL` No XENIX system semaphores available	An `opensem`(2), `waitsem`(2), or `sigsem`(2) was issued to a XENIX system semaphore that has not been initialized by a call to `creatsem`(2). A `sigsem` was issued to a XENIX system semaphore out of sequence; that is, before the process has issued the corresponding `waitsem` to the semaphore. An `nbwaitsem` was issued to a semaphore guarding a resource that is currently in use by another process. The semaphore that a process was waiting on has been left in an inconsistent state when the process controlling the semaphore exited without relinquishing control properly; that is, without issuing a `waitsem` on the semaphore

Table A-1 *System Call Errors (Continued)*

No.	name summary	Meaning
139	`EISNAM` Is a XENIX system named type file	An attempt was made to perform an operation not appropriate for a XENIX system "named" file, such as `open`(2).
143	`ESHUTDOWN` Can't send after transport endpoint shutdown	A request to send data was disallowed because the transport endpoint has already been shut down.
144	`ETOOMANYREFS`	There are too many references; cannot splice.
145	`ETIMEOUT` Connection timed out	A connect or send request failed because the connected party did not properly respond after a period of time. The timeout period is dependent on the communication protocol.
146	`ECONNREFUSED` Connection refused	No connection could be made because the target machine actively refused it. The error usually results from trying to connect to a service that is inactive on the remote host.
147	`EHOSTDOWN` Host is down	A transport provider operation failed because the destination host was down.
148	`EHOSTUNREACH` No route to host	A transport provider operation was attempted to an unreachable host.
149	`EALREADY` Operation already in progress	An operation was attempted on a non-blocking object that already had an operation in progress.
150	`EINPROGRESS` Operation now in progress	An operation that takes a long time to complete (such as `connect`) was attempted on a non-blocking object.
151	`ESTALE`	Encountered stale NFS file handle.
152	`ENOLOAD`	Could not load the required loadable module.
153	`ERELOC`	Relocation error occurred when module was being loaded.
154	`ENOMATCH`	No symbol matched the given specification.
156	`EBADVER`	A version number mismatch occurred.
157	`ECONFIG`	The configured kernel resource was exhausted.

B

Signal References

This appendix provides, for your convenience, tables summarizing pertinent information relating to signals.

- `signal.h` facility
- `siginfo.h` facility
- `sigaction` system call
- `sigaltstack` system call

signal.h

A signal is an asynchronous notification of an event, such as a hardware fault, timer expiration, terminal activity, invocation of the `kill` or `sigsend` system calls.

Table B-1 lists the signals currently defined in `sys/signal.h`.

Table B-1 *Signals Defined in* `sys/signal.h`

Name	Value	Default	Event
SIGHUP	1	Exit	Hangup [see termio(7)]
SIGINT	2	Exit	Interrupt [see termio(7)]
SIGQUIT	3	Core	Quit [see termio(7)]
SIGILL	4	Core	Illegal instruction
SIGTRAP	5	Core	Trace/Breakpoint trap
SIGABRT	6	Core	Abort
SIGEMT	7	Core	Emulation trap
SIGFPE	8	Core	Arithmetic exception
SIGKILL	9	Exit	Killed; cannot be altered or blocked
SIGBUS	10	Core	Bus error
SIGSEGV	11	Core	Segmentation fault
SIGSYS	12	Core	Bad system call
SIGPIPE	13	Exit	Broken pipe
SIGALRM	14	Exit	Alarm clock
SIGTERM	15	Exit	Terminated
SIGUSR1	16	Exit	User signal 1
SIGUSR2	17	Exit	User signal 2
SIGCHILD	18	Ignore	Child status
SIGPWR	19	Ignore	Power fail/restart
SIGWINCH	20	Ignore	Window size change
SIGURG	21	Ignore	Urgent socket condition
SIGPOLL	22	Ignore	Socket I/O possible
SIGSTOP	23	Stop	Stopped (signal); cannot be altered or blocked
SIGTSTP	24	Stop	Stopped (user) [see termio(7)]
SIGCONT	25	Ignore	Continued
SIGTTIN	26	Stop	Stopped (tty input) [see termio(7)]
SIGTTOU	27	Stop	Stopped (tty output) [see termio(7)]
SIGVTALRM	28	Exit	Virtual timer expired
SIGPROF	29	Exit	Profiling timer expired
SIGXCPU	30	Core	CPU time limit exceeded [see getrlimit(2)]
SIGXFSZ	31	Core	File size limit exceeded [see getrlimit(2)]

The default actions are defined as follows.

Exit — Upon receipt of signal, the receiving process is to be terminated with all the consequences outlined in `exit` (2).

Core — Upon receipt of signal, the receiving process is to be terminated with all the consequences outlined in `exit` (2). In addition, a core image of the process is constructed in the current working directory.

Stop — Upon receipt of signal, the receiving process is to stop.

Ignore — Upon receipt of signal, the receiving process is to ignore the signal. (Equivalent to setting disposition to `SIG_IGN`.)

siginfo.h

A process that is catching a signal may request information about why the system generated that signal. `si_code`, contained in a structure of type `siginfo_t`, contains a signal-specific reason why the signal was generated. Table B-1 summarizes the codes.

Table B-2 *Signal Code Defined by* `si_code`

Signal	Code	Reason
SIGILL	ILL_ILLOPC	Illegal opcode
	ILL_ILLOPN	Illegal operand
	ILL_ILLADR	Illegal addressing mode
	ILL_ILLTRP	Illegal trap
	ILL_PRVOPC	Privileged opcode
	ILL_PRVREG	Privileged register
	ILL_COPROC	Co-processor error
	ILL_BADSTK	Internal stack error
SIGFPE	FPE_INTDIV	Integer divide by zero
	FPE_INTOVF	Integer overflow
	FPE_FLTDIV	Floating point divide by zero
	FPE_FLTOVF	Floating point overflow
	FPE_FLTUND	Floating point underflow
	FPE_FLTRES	Floating point inexact result
	FPE_FLTINV	Invalid floating point operation
	FPE_FPESUB	Subscript out of range
SIGSEGV	SEGV_MAPERR	Address not mapped to object
	SEGV_ACCERR	Invalid permissions for mapped object

Table B-2 *Signal Code Defined by `si_code` (Continued)*

Signal	Code	Reason
SIGBUS	BUS_ADRALN	Invalid address alignment
	BUS_ADRERR	Non-existent physical address
	BUS_OBJERR	Object-specific hardware error
SIGTRAP	TRAP_BRKPT	Process breakpoint
	TRAP_TRACE	Process trace trap
SIGCHILD	CLD_EXITED	Child has exited
	CLD_KILLED	Child was killed
	CLD_DUMPED	Child terminated abnormally
	CLD_TRAPPED	Traced child has trapped
	CLD_STOPPED	Child has stopped
	CLD_CONTINUED	Stopped child had continued
SIGPOLL	POLL_IN	Data input available
	POLL_OUT	Output buffers available
	POLL_MSG	Input message available
	POLL_ERR	I/O error
	POLL_PRI	High priority input available
	POLL_HUP	Device disconnected

If the value of `si_code` is less than or equal to zero, then the signal was generated by a user process [see `kill`(2) and `sigsend`(2)] and the `siginfo` structure contains the following additional information:

```
pid_t si_pid          /* sending process ID */
uid_t si_uid          /* sending user ID */
```

sigaction

`sigaction` provides detailed signal management, allowing the calling process to examine and specify the action to be taken on delivery of a specific signal.

`sigaction` has the form

```
#include <signal.h>

int sigaction(int sig, const struct sigaction *act,
   struct sigaction *oact);
```

The sigaction structure includes the following members:

```
void            (*sa_handler)();
sigset_t        sa_mask;
int             sa_flags;
```

sa_handler
: Specifies the disposition of the signal and may take any of the values specified in signal (see Table B-1).

sa_mask
: Specifies a set of signals to be blocked while the signal handler is active. SIGSTOP and SIGKILL cannot be blocked.

sa_flags
: Specifies a set of flags that modify the delivery of the signal. It is formed by a logical OR of the values listed in Table B-3.

Table B-3 ***sa_flags in sigaction***

sa_flags	Meaning
SA_ONSTACK	If set and the signal is caught and an alternate signal stack has been declared with sigaltstack(2), then the signal is delivered to the calling process on that stack. Otherwise, the signal should be delivered on the current stack.
SA_RESETHAND	If set and the signal is caught, then the disposition of the signal is reset to SIG_DFL, and the signal will not be blocked on entry to the signal handler. SIGILL, SIGTRAP, and SIGPWR cannot be automatically reset when delivered.
SA_NODEFER	If set and the signal is caught, then the signal will not be automatically blocked by the kernel while it is being caught.
SA_RESTART	If set and the signal is caught, then a system call that is interrupted by the execution of this signal's handler is transparently restarted by the system. Otherwise, that system call returns an EINTR error.

Table B-3 *sa_flags in sigaction (Continued)*

sa_flags	Meaning
SA_SIGINFO	If cleared and the signal is caught, then *sig* is passed as the only argument to the signal-catching function. If set and the signal is caught, then two additional arguments are passed to the signal-catching function. If the second argument is not equal to NULL, then it points to a siginfo_t structure containing the reason why the signal was generated (see Table B-1.). The third argument points to a ucontext_t structure containing the receiving process's context when the signal was delivered [see ucontext(5)].
SA_NOCLDWAIT	If set and *sig* equals SIGCHLD, then the system will not create zombie processes when children of the calling process exit. If the calling process subsequently issues a wait(2), then it blocks until all of the calling process's child processes terminate, when it returns a value of -1 with errno set to ECHILD.
SA_NOCLDSTOP	If set and *sig* equal SIGCHLD, then *sig* will not be sent to the calling process when its child processes stop or continue.

On success, sigaction returns zero. On failure, it returns -1 and sets errno to indicate the error.

sigaltstack

sigaltstack allows you to define an alternate stack area on which signals are to be processed. sigaltstack is specified with a sigaction call (see Table B-3). sigaltstack has the form

```
#include <signal.h>

int sigaltstack(const stack_t *ss, stack_t *oss);
```

The sigaltstack structure includes the following members:

```
char        *ss_sp
int         ss_size
int         ss_flags
```

ss_sp and ss_size
Specify the new base and size of the stack, which is automatically adjusted for direction of growth and alignment.

ss_flags Specifies the stack's state and can contain the values listed in Table B-4.

Table B-4 ***ss_flags in sigaltstack***

If	then ss_flags	Means
ss is not NULL	SS_DISABLE	The stack is to be disabled and ss_sp and ss_size are ignored. If SS_DISABLE is not set, then the stack is enabled. SS_DISABLE is the only way you can disable the alternate signal stack.
oss is not NULL	SS_ONSTACK	The process is currently executing on the alternate signal stack. Attempts to modify the alternate signal stack while the process is executing on it will fail. You cannot modify SS_ONSTACK.
oss is not NULL	SS_DISABLE	The alternate signal stack is currently disabled.

On success, sigaltstack returns zero. On failure, it returns -1 and sets errno to indicate the error.

Glossary

`a.out` Historically, for "assembler output." The default file name for an executable program produced by the C compilation system.

access permission
Authorization to gain access to an object for certain purposes, such as to read, write, and/or to execute/search. Access checking is performed whenever a subject (a process) tries to access an object (such as a file or directory). Permission to access an object is granted or denied on the basis of mode bits known as Discretionary Access Control (DAC).

ANSI American National Standards Institute. ANSI establishes standards in the computing industry from the definition of ASCII (see below) to the measurement of overall datacom system performance. ANSI standards have been established for the Ada, FORTRAN, and C programming languages.

API Application programmer interface.

application An executable program, usually unique to one type of users' work, such as an accounting application. Applications are frequently interactive environments in which the user can perform various related tasks.

archive A statically linked library; a collection of object files each of which contains the code for a function or a group of related functions in the library. When a library function is called in a program and a static linking option is specified on the `cc` command line, a copy of the object file that contains the function is incorporated in the executable at link time.

argument A character string or number that follows a command and controls its execution in some way. There are two types of arguments: options and operands. ***Options*** change the execution or output of the command. Options are also called ***flags***. ***Operands*** provide data that will be operated on by the command. Operands specify files or directories to be operated on by the program.

In the C language, function arguments are enclosed in a pair of parentheses immediately following the function name. Formal definitions of the functions are supplied with the C compilation system in `cc(1)`.

ASCII American Standard Code for Information Interchange. ASCII code uses one byte of computer memory to represent each character. Each alphanumeric and special character has an ASCII equivalent. When files and directories are printed according to the ASCII code equivalent of the first letter of their names, the order is called ASCII collating sequence. The order is special characters first, numbers second, then upper case and lower case letters.

assembler A programming language that uses symbolic names to represent the machine instructions of a given computer. An assembler is a program that accepts instructions written in the assembly language of the computer and translates them into a binary representation of the corresponding machine instructions. Because each assembly language instruction usually has a one-to-one correspondence with a machine instruction, programs written in assembly language are not portable to different machines.

base address

The difference between the virtual address of any segment in memory and the corresponding virtual address in an object file; thus, a single constant value for any one executable or shared object in a given process. One use of the base address is to relocate the memory image of a program during dynamic linking.

buffer A space in computer memory where data is stored temporarily in convenient units for system operations. Buffers are often used by programs such as editors that access and alter text or data frequently. For example, when a user edits a file, a copy of its contents are read into a buffer; the copy is what the user changes. Changes become part of the permanent file when the user writes the buffer's contents back into the permanent file, replacing the contents of the file with the contents of the buffer.

callback A routine written by an application programmer and associated with a specific widget *resource*. The callback routine is invoked as a result of a specific activity associated with that widget; that is, the widget calls back the program via that routine. For example, the `XtNselect` *resource* contains the name of the callback routine that is entered when a *button* is pushed or when a `CheckBox` is selected; the `XtNverification` resource contains the name of the callback routine to invoke when a `TextField` widget is exited. The act of associating the name of a callback routine with a widget resource is called *registration*.

character Any bit pattern able to fit into a byte on the machine. (A multibyte character is an exception to the definition.)

character class table
A table used for character classification and conversion. The table is built by the commands `chrtbl`(1M) and `wchrtbl(1M)`, and located in the file `usr/lib/`*locale*`/LC_CTYPE`.

child process
See *`fork`*().

COFF Common object file format. A file format replaced by Executable and Linking Format (ELF).

command One of a set of executables built into FMLI, such as `open` and `close`, to which descriptors of type command must evaluate. A command line consists of the command followed by its arguments. For example:

```
$ cc file1.c file2.c
```

instructs the operating system to execute the C compiler program, which is stored in the file `cc`, and to use the source files `file1.c` and `file2.c` as input. A command line can extend over multiple terminal lines.

compiler A program that translates a source program written in a higher-level language into the assembly language of the computer on which the program is to run. An assembler translates the assembly language code into the machine instructions of the computer. In the C compilation system, the instructions are stored in object files that correspond to each source file. Each object file contains a binary representation of the C language code in the corresponding source file. The link editor links these object files with each other and with any library functions used in the source code to produce an executable program, called `a.out` by default.

core image A copy of the memory image of a process. A file named `core` is created in a user's current directory when the UNIX operating system aborts an executing program. The file contains an image of the process at the time of the failure.

daemon A background process that performs a system-wide public function. The UNIX operating system process `init` may spawn daemon processes that exist throughout the lifetime of the system. Daemons (often) continue to run after their parents terminate. An example of a daemon process is `calendar(1)`.

data symbol
Names a variable that might or might not be initialized. Normally, these variables reside in read/write memory during execution. Compare *text symbol*.

debugging The process of locating and correcting errors in executable programs.

default The way a program performs a task in the absence of other instructions; that is, in default of a programmer specifying something else.

directory A type of file used to group and organize other files or directories. A subdirectory is a directory that is pointed to by a directory one level above it in the file system. A directory name is a string of characters that identifies the directory. It can be a simple directory name, a relative path name, or a full path name.

display width
The width in screen columns required to display the characters of a particular code set. Display width is defined in the character class table.

downstream
In a stream, the direction from stream head to driver.

driver In a stream, provides the interface between peripheral hardware and the stream. A driver can also be a pseudo-driver, such as a multiplexor or log driver [see `log`(7)], which is not associated with a hardware device.

dynamic linking
The process in which external references in a program are linked with their definitions when the program is executed.

ELF Executable and Linking Format. The format of the object files produced by the C compilation system in System V Release 4.

error message
A response from a program indicating that a problem has arisen or that something unexpected has happened that requires attention.

`exec`(2) A system call that overlays a new process image on an old process. The new process image is constructed from an ordinary executable file, which is either an executable object file or a file of data for an interpreter. Because the calling process image is overlaid by the new process image, no return from a successful `exec` is possible.

executable file
A type of object file that holds a program suitable for execu-

tion. The file specifies how a program's process image is to be created.

executable program
On the UNIX operating system, a compiled and linked program or a shell program. The command to execute either program is the name of the file containing the program. Compare *object file*.

executable A program that can be processed or executed by the computer without any further translation; a file that has execute permission, such as an `a.out` file or a shell script.

expression A mathematical or logical symbol or meaningful combination of symbols.

FALSE A value to which a Boolean descriptor can evaluate. FALSE must be the word "false," irrespective of case, or a non-zero return code.

File Class Database
A database containing file class definitions, where each definition consists of a file class name and a list of properties. The properties define the visual and metaphor behavior of files belonging to the file class.

file descriptor
An integer value assigned by the operating system to a file when the file is opened by a process.

file system type
Each different file system implementation that is incorporated into the VFS architecture. A file system type may support different file types. The traditional System V file system type, a secure file system type, a high performance file system type, and an MS-DOS file system type are examples of possible file system types.

file system In the UNIX operating system, a hierarchical collection of directories and other files that are organized in a tree structure. The base of the structure is the root (/) directory; other directories, all subordinate to root, are branches. The collection of files can be mounted on a block special file. Each file of a file system appears exactly once in the inode list of the file system and is accessible via a single, unique path from the root directory of the file system.

file type The determinant of the general, expected characteristics of a file. File types include regular file, character special file, block special file, FIFO, directory, and symbolic link. Each file type is supported within some file system type

file A potential source of input or a potential destination for output; at some point, then, an identifiable collection of information. A file is known to the UNIX operating system as an inode plus the information the inode contains that tells whether the file is a plain file, a special file, or a directory. A plain file contains text, data, programs, or other information that forms a coherent unit. A special file is a hardware device or portion thereof, such as a disk partition. A directory is a type of file that contains the names and inode addresses of other plain, special, or directory files.

flag See *argument*.

`fork`() A system call that splits one process into two, the parent process and the child process, with separate, but initially identical, text, data, and stack segments. See `fork`(2) for more information.

form field An area of a form consisting of a field label and a field input area into which a user can enter information.

fundamental block size
The minimal file allocation unit. In the case of disk-based file systems this is a disk sector or a multiple of disk sectors, smaller than or equal to the preferred block size (see below).

global symbol
A symbol that is visible to all object files being combined. One file's definition of a global symbol will satisfy another file's undefined reference to the same global symbol.

header file A file that usually contains shared data declarations that are to be copied into source files by the compiler. Header file names conventionally end with the characters `.h`. Header files are also called include files, for the C language `#include` directive by which they are made available to source files.

I/O Input/output. The process by which information enters (input) and leaves (output) a computer system.

include file
See *header file*.

interpreter A program that allows communication with the operating system. It reads entered commands and interprets them as requests to execute other programs, access files, or provide output.

interrupt A signal generated by a hardware condition or peripheral device. For example, typing a break character on a terminal generates an interrupt that terminates the user process connected to the terminal.

kernel The basic resident software of the UNIX operating system. The kernel is responsible for most system operations: scheduling and managing the work done by the computer, maintaining the file system, and so forth. The kernel has its own text, data, and stack areas.

lexical analysis
The process by which a stream of characters (often comprising a source program) is broken up into its elementary words and symbols, called tokens. The tokens can include the reserved words of a programming language, its identifiers and constants, and special symbols such as `=`, `:=`, and `;`. In compilers, a lexical analyzer is often called by a syntactic analyzer, or parser, that analyzes the grammatical form of tokens passed to it by the lexical analyzer.

library A file that contains object code for a group of commonly used functions. Rather than writing the functions, a programmer arranges for the functions to be linked with a program when an executable is created (see *archive*) or when it is run (see *shared object*).

link editing
The process in which a symbol referenced in one module of a program is connected with its definition in another. With the C compilation system, programs are linked either statically when an executable is created, or dynamically when the executable is run.

local symbol
A symbol that is not visible outside the object file containing its definition. Local symbols of the same name may exist in multiple files without interfering with each other.

makefile A file that is used with the program `make` to keep track of the dependencies between modules of a program, so that when one module is changed, dependent ones are brought up to date.

module A program component that typically contains a function or a group of related functions. Source files and libraries are modules.

null pointer
In the C language, a pointer with a value of 0.

object file A file containing a binary representation of programming language code. A relocatable object file contains references to symbols that have not yet been linked with their definitions. An executable object file is a linked program. Compare *source file*.

onstop event
A notification to the debugger to perform a specified action whenever a process stops for any reason. The action is one or more of the commands available through the debugger's command line interface.

operand See *argument*.

optimizer A facility that improves the efficiency of the assembly language code generated by a compiler. That improvement in turn speeds the execution time of object code.

option See *argument*.

page A fixed length, 1024-byte block that has a virtual address and that can be transferred between main and secondary storage.

paging The process by which programs are broken into pages and transferred between main and secondary storage by the paging daemon.

parent process
See `fork()`.

parser A syntactic analyzer that analyzes the grammatical form of tokens passed to it by a lexical analyzer (see *lexical analysis*).

path name A locator of a file in the file system, made up of a series of directory names that proceed down the hierarchical path of the file system. The directory names are separated by a slash character (`/`). The last name in the path is the file. If the path name begins with a slash, it is called an absolute, or full, path name; the initial slash means that the path begins at the root directory. A path name that does not begin with a slash is known as a relative path name, meaning relative to a user's current directory.

PID Process ID; an integer that identifies a process.

ping A call to procedure `0` of an RPC program. Pinging is used to verify the existence and accessibility of a remote program. Pinging can also be used to time network communications.

pipe The case in which the output of one program is used as the input to another program, so that the programs run in sequence. A pipeline is created by preceding each command after the first command with the pipe symbol (`|`), which indicates that the output from the process on the left should be routed to the process on the right. For example,

```
$ who | wc -l
```

causes the output of the `who` command, which lists the users who are logged in to the system, to be used as the input of the `wc`, or word count, command with the `-l` option. The result is the number of users logged in to the system.

pixel An addressable point on the screen.

pixmap A bitmap of an area of the screen stored within the program. Also, a defined data type in the Xt Intrinsics.

portability The degree of ease with which a program can be moved, or ported, to a different operating system or machine.

preferred block size
The unit of transfer for block devices in read/write operations (also known as "logical block size").

preprocessor
A program that prepares an input file for another program. The preprocessor component of the C compiler performs macro expansion, conditional compilation, and file inclusion.

`/proc` directory
A file system that provides access to an image of each active process in the system. The name of an entry in a `/proc` directory is a decimal number corresponding to the process ID.

process An instance of a program being executed. A number that identifies an active process. In the UNIX operating system, a process incorporates the concept of an execution environment, including contents of memory, register values, name of the current directory, status of files, and various other information.

process ID An integer that identifies a process. See `ps`(1) for more information on how to determine the process ID of any process currently active on a system.

process image
A dynamic program representation, produced by the dynamic linker; the combination of an executable file and other shared objects.

program A set of instructions and data kept in an ordinary file.

program header table
An array of structures, each describing a segment or other information the system needs to prepare a program for execution.

read queue In a stream, the message queue in a module or driver containing messages moving upstream.

register, registration
To make a routine name known to the API. When the application programmer develops a *callback* routine, that routine must be registered when the widget is created so that it can be properly invoked.

regular expression
A string of alphanumeric characters and special characters that describes, in a shorthand way, a pattern to be searched for in a file.

relocatable file
A type of object file that holds code and data suitable for linking with other object files to create an executable or a shared object file.

relocation The process of connecting symbolic references with symbolic definitions. For example, when a program calls a function, the associated call instruction must transfer control to the proper destination address at execution.

relocation entry
Information that describes how to modify the section contents of a relocatable file, thus allowing executable and shared object files to hold the correct information for a process's program image.

resource translation
The mechanism by which resource values are made accessible to widgets. The list of resources is contained in the `app-defaults` files. Each entry in these files consists of a resource name/value pair of the form: *app_name.resource_-name*: *value*. Using an asterisk in place of the *app_name* makes the entry available to any application that recognizes the *resource_name*. Any hard-coded value takes precedence over what is set in the resource file.

resource An attribute of a widget or a widget class. A named data value in the defining structure of a widget.

root directory
The origin of the directory hierarchy in a file system, called "/" by convention. Each process has associated with it a concept of a root directory and a current directory for the purpose of resolving path name searches. The root directory of a process need not be the root directory of the root file system.

routine Another name for a function in C.

RPC language
A C-like programming language recognized by the `rpcgen` compiler.

RPC Package
The collection of software and documentation used to implement and support remote procedure calls in System V. The RPC Package implements and is a superset of the functionality of the RPC Protocol.

RPC Protocol
The message-passing protocol that is the basis of the RPC package.

RPC/XDR See *RPC language.*

search path An ordered list of directory path names that will be prefixed to command names until the path name of an executable file results. The search path is specified in the PATH environment variable.

semaphore identifier (`semid`)
A unique positive integer created by a `semget` system call. Each `semid` has a set of semaphores and a data structure associated with it.

server The transport user in connection-mode that offers services to other users (clients) and enables these clients to establish a transport connection to it.

service indication
The notification of a pending event generated by the provider to a user of a particular service.

service primitive
The unit of information passed across a service interface that contains either a service request or service indication.

service request
A request for some action generated by a user to the provider of a particular service.

session ID A positive integer that is the unique identifier of a session during its lifetime.

session leader
A process whose session ID is the same as its process and process group ID.

session lifetime
The duration from the time a session is created by its session leader to the time when the last process that is a member of the session ends, or when the last process that is a member in the session leaves the session.

session A group of processes identified by a common ID called a session ID, capable of establishing a connection with a controlling terminal. Any process that is not a process group leader can create a new session and process group, becoming the session leader of the session and process group leader of the process group. A newly created process joins the session of its creator.

shared memory identifier (`shmid`)
A unique positive integer created by a `shmget` system call. Each `shmid` has a segment of memory (referred to as a shared memory segment) and a data structure associated with it. (Note that these shared memory segments must be explicitly removed by the user after the last reference to them is removed.)

shared object
A dynamically linked library that is a single object file containing the code for every function in the library. When a library function is called in a program and a dynamic linking option is specified on the `cc` command line, the entire contents of the shared object are mapped into the virtual address space of the process at runtime. As its name implies, a shared object contains code that can be used simultaneously by different programs at runtime.

shared object file
A type of object file that holds code and data suitable for linking in two contexts. First, the link editor processes the shared object file with other relocatable and shared object files to create another object file. Second, the dynamic linker combines it with an executable file and other shared objects to create a process image.

shell The UNIX system program that handles communication between users and the system. The shell is known as a command interpreter because it translates commands into a language understandable by the system. A shell normally is started when a user logs in to the system. A shell program calls the shell to read and execute commands contained in an executable file.

signal An asynchronous notification of an event. A message that a user sends to a process or that processes send to one another. One might use a signal, for example, to initiate an interrupt.

A signal sent by a running process is usually a sign of an exceptional occurrence that has caused the process to terminate or divert from the normal flow of control.

simplified interface
The simplest level of the RPC package.

source file A file containing the programming language version of a program. Before a computer can execute the program, the source code must be translated by a compiler and assembler into the machine language of the computer. Compare *object file*.

special processes
Process with ID 0 and ID 1, referred to as proc0 and proc1; see `kill`(2). proc0 is the process scheduler. proc1 is the initialization process (`init`); proc1 is the ancestor of every other process in the system and is used to control the process structure.

standard error
An output stream from a program that normally is used to convey error messages. In the UNIX operating system, the default case is to associate standard error with the user's terminal.

standard input
An input stream to a program. In the UNIX operating system, the default case is to associate standard input with the user's terminal.

standard output
An output stream from a program. On the UNIX operating system, the default case is to associate standard output with the user's terminal.

static data A condition persistent throughout a process. Static data occupies the `data` segment and the `bss` segment.

static linking
The process in which external references in a program are linked with their definitions when an executable is created.

stream A full-duplex data path within the kernel between a user process and driver routines. The primary components are a stream head, a driver, and zero or more modules between the stream head and driver. A stream is analogous to a shell pipeline except that data flow and processing are bidirectional.

stream head
The end of the stream. Provides the interface between the stream and a user process. The principal functions of the stream head are processing STREAMS-related system calls, and passing data and information between a user process and the stream.

STREAMS A set of kernel mechanisms that support the development of network services and data communication drivers. It defines interface standards for character input/output within the kernel and between the kernel and user level processes. The STREAMS mechanism is composed of utility routines, kernel facilities, and a set of data structures.

string A contiguous sequence of characters treated as a unit. In the C language, a character string is an array of characters terminated by the null character, `\0`.

SVID System V Interface Definition. Defines the standard interface for SVR4 and is the basis of other UNIX operating system standards.

swap To move the core image of an executing program between main memory and secondary storage to make room for other processes.

syntax 1) The order in which commands and their arguments must be put together. The command always comes first. The order of arguments varies from command to command. 2) The set of rules that describes how the elements of a programming language may legally be used.

system call A request from a program for an action to be performed by the UNIX operating system kernel.

templates Files that are used as the initial structure and/or content of newly created files. Template files are specified for each file class by the TEMPLATES class property. (OEMs and ISVs can add new templates.)

text symbol
Names a program instruction. Instructions reside in read-only memory during execution. Compare *data symbol.*

toggle An action performed on an object with two states that switches the object from one state to the other.

trap A method of detecting and interpreting certain hardware and software conditions by means of software. A trap is set to catch a signal or interrupt in order to determine what course of action to take.

TRUE A value to which a Boolean descriptor can evaluate. Any value other than those defined for FALSE is interpreted as TRUE.

`truss`(1) A system command for tracing system calls, signals, and machine faults.

UFS Unified File System. A derivative of the 4.2BSD file system. UFS offers file hardening, supports large and fragmented block allocations for files, distributed inode and free block management, and quotas.

universal address
A machine-independent representation of a network address.

upstream In a stream, the direction from driver to stream head.

user ID An integer value, usually associated with a login name, that the system uses to identify owners of files and directories. The user ID of a process becomes the owner of files created by the process and by descendant processes.

variable In a program, an object whose value may change during the execution of the program or from one execution to the next. A variable in the shell is a name representing a string of characters.

Vnode The operating system's internal representation of a file (previously known as a file-system-independent inode).

virtual memory
A mechanism that permits programs to treat disk storage as an extension of main memory.

weak symbol
A symbol that, like a global symbol, is visible to all object files being combined. It has lower precedence than a global symbol.

X/Open The X/Open Company Limited. A consortium of computer firms dedicated to achieving open UNIX systems.

XDR language
A protocol specification language for data representation. RPC language builds on and is a superset of XDR.

XDR eXternal Data Representation. Provides an architecture independent representation of data.

zombie process
A process that only occupies a slot in the process table. It has no other space allocated either in user or kernel space. It is created when a terminated calling process is transformed to a zombie process because its parent process has not specified the `SA_NOCLDWAIT` flag.

Index

Files

F

G

H

I

L

M

N

O

P

R

S

W

Z